German Literature: A Very Short Introduction

VERY SHORT INTRODUCTIONS are for anyone wanting a stimulating and accessible way in to a new subject. They are written by experts, and have been published in more than 25 languages worldwide.

The series began in 1995, and now represents a wide variety of topics in history, philosophy, religion, science, and the humanities. Over the next few years it will grow to a library of around 200 volumes – a Very Short Introduction to everything from ancient Egypt and Indian philosophy to conceptual art and cosmology.

Very Short Introductions available now:

AFRICAN HISTORY
    John Parker and Richard Rathbone
AMERICAN POLITICAL PARTIES
    AND ELECTIONS L. Sandy Maisel
THE AMERICAN PRESIDENCY
    Charles O. Jones
ANARCHISM Colin Ward
ANCIENT EGYPT Ian Shaw
ANCIENT PHILOSOPHY Julia Annas
ANCIENT WARFARE
    Harry Sidebottom
ANGLICANISM Mark Chapman
THE ANGLO-SAXON AGE John Blair
ANIMAL RIGHTS David DeGrazia
ANTISEMITISM Steven Beller
ARCHAEOLOGY Paul Bahn
ARCHITECTURE Andrew Ballantyne
ARISTOTLE Jonathan Barnes
ART HISTORY Dana Arnold
ART THEORY Cynthia Freeland
THE HISTORY OF ASTRONOMY
    Michael Hoskin
ATHEISM Julian Baggini
AUGUSTINE Henry Chadwick
BARTHES Jonathan Culler
BESTSELLERS John Sutherland
THE BIBLE John Riches
THE BRAIN Michael O'Shea
BRITISH POLITICS Anthony Wright
BUDDHA Michael Carrithers
BUDDHISM Damien Keown
BUDDHIST ETHICS Damien Keown
CAPITALISM James Fulcher
THE CELTS Barry Cunliffe

CHAOS Leonard Smith
CHOICE THEORY Michael Allingham
CHRISTIAN ART Beth Williamson
CHRISTIANITY Linda Woodhead
CLASSICS
    Mary Beard and John Henderson
CLASSICAL MYTHOLOGY
    Helen Morales
CLAUSEWITZ Michael Howard
THE COLD WAR Robert McMahon
CONSCIOUSNESS Susan Blackmore
CONTEMPORARY ART
    Julian Stallabrass
CONTINENTAL PHILOSOPHY
    Simon Critchley
COSMOLOGY Peter Coles
THE CRUSADES Christopher Tyerman
CRYPTOGRAPHY
    Fred Piper and Sean Murphy
DADA AND SURREALISM
    David Hopkins
DARWIN Jonathan Howard
THE DEAD SEA SCROLLS Timothy Lim
DEMOCRACY Bernard Crick
DESCARTES Tom Sorell
DESIGN John Heskett
DINOSAURS David Norman
DOCUMENTARY FILM
    Patricia Aufderheide
DREAMING J. Allan Hobson
DRUGS Leslie Iversen
THE EARTH Martin Redfern
ECONOMICS Partha Dasgupta
EGYPTIAN MYTH Geraldine Pinch

EIGHTEENTH-CENTURY BRITAIN
Paul Langford
THE ELEMENTS Philip Ball
EMOTION Dylan Evans
EMPIRE Stephen Howe
ENGELS Terrell Carver
ETHICS Simon Blackburn
THE EUROPEAN UNION
John Pinder and Simon Usherwood
EVOLUTION
Brian and Deborah Charlesworth
EXISTENTIALISM Thomas Flynn
FASCISM Kevin Passmore
FEMINISM Margaret Walters
THE FIRST WORLD WAR
Michael Howard
FOSSILS Keith Thomson
FOUCAULT Gary Gutting
THE FRENCH REVOLUTION
William Doyle
FREE WILL Thomas Pink
FREUD Anthony Storr
FUNDAMENTALISM Malise Ruthven
GALAXIES John Gribbin
GALILEO Stillman Drake
GAME THEORY Ken Binmore
GANDHI Bhikhu Parekh
GEOPOLITICS Klaus Dodds
GERMAN LITERATURE Nicholas Boyle
GLOBAL CATASTROPHES Bill McGuire
GLOBALIZATION Manfred Steger
GLOBAL WARMING Mark Maslin
THE GREAT DEPRESSION AND THE
NEW DEAL Eric Rauchway
HABERMAS James Gordon Finlayson
HEGEL Peter Singer
HEIDEGGER Michael Inwood
HIEROGLYPHS Penelope Wilson
HINDUISM Kim Knott
HISTORY John H. Arnold
HIV/AIDS Alan Whiteside
HOBBES Richard Tuck
HUMAN EVOLUTION Bernard Wood
HUMAN RIGHTS Andrew Clapham
HUME A. J. Ayer
IDEOLOGY Michael Freeden
INDIAN PHILOSOPHY Sue Hamilton
INTELLIGENCE Ian J. Deary
INTERNATIONAL MIGRATION
Khalid Koser

INTERNATIONAL RELATIONS
Paul Wilkinson
ISLAM Malise Ruthven
JOURNALISM Ian Hargreaves
JUDAISM Norman Solomon
JUNG Anthony Stevens
KABBALAH Joseph Dan
KAFKA Ritchie Robertson
KANT Roger Scruton
KIERKEGAARD Patrick Gardiner
THE KORAN Michael Cook
LAW Raymond Wacks
LINGUISTICS Peter Matthews
LITERARY THEORY Jonathan Culler
LOCKE John Dunn
LOGIC Graham Priest
MACHIAVELLI Quentin Skinner
THE MARQUIS DE SADE John Phillips
MARX Peter Singer
MATHEMATICS Timothy Gowers
MEDICAL ETHICS Tony Hope
MEDIEVAL BRITAIN John Gillingham
and Ralph A. Griffiths
MODERN ART David Cottington
MODERN CHINA Rana Mitter
MODERN IRELAND Senia Pašeta
MOLECULES Philip Ball
MUSIC Nicholas Cook
MYTH Robert A. Segal
NATIONALISM Steven Grosby
THE NEW TESTAMENT AS
LITERATURE Kyle Keefer
NEWTON Robert Iliffe
NIETZSCHE Michael Tanner
NINETEENTH-CENTURY BRITAIN
Christopher Harvie and
H. C. G. Matthew
NORTHERN IRELAND
Marc Mulholland
NUCLEAR WEAPONS
Joseph M. Siracusa
PARTICLE PHYSICS Frank Close
PAUL E. P. Sanders
PHILOSOPHY Edward Craig
PHILOSOPHY OF LAW
Raymond Wacks
PHILOSOPHY OF SCIENCE
Samir Okasha
PHOTOGRAPHY Steve Edwards
PLATO Julia Annas

POLITICS Kenneth Minogue
POLITICAL PHILOSOPHY
David Miller
POSTCOLONIALISM Robert Young
POSTMODERNISM Christopher Butler
POSTSTRUCTURALISM
Catherine Belsey
PREHISTORY Chris Gosden
PRESOCRATIC PHILOSOPHY
Catherine Osborne
PSYCHOLOGY Gillian Butler and
Freda McManus
PSYCHIATRY Tom Burns
THE QUAKERS Pink Dandelion
QUANTUM THEORY
John Polkinghorne
RACISM Ali Rattansi
THE RENAISSANCE Jerry Brotton
RENAISSANCE ART
Geraldine A. Johnson
ROMAN BRITAIN Peter Salway
THE ROMAN EMPIRE
Christopher Kelly
ROUSSEAU Robert Wokler
RUSSELL A. C. Grayling
RUSSIAN LITERATURE Catriona Kelly
THE RUSSIAN REVOLUTION
S. A. Smith

SCHIZOPHRENIA
Chris Frith and Eve Johnstone
SCHOPENHAUER Christopher Janaway
SHAKESPEARE Germaine Greer
SIKHISM Eleanor Nesbitt
SOCIAL AND CULTURAL
ANTHROPOLOGY
John Monaghan and Peter Just
SOCIALISM Michael Newman
SOCIOLOGY Steve Bruce
SOCRATES C. C. W. Taylor
THE SPANISH CIVIL WAR
Helen Graham
SPINOZA Roger Scruton
STUART BRITAIN John Morrill
TERRORISM Charles Townshend
THEOLOGY David F. Ford
THE HISTORY OF TIME
Leofranc Holford-Strevens
TRAGEDY Adrian Poole
THE TUDORS John Guy
TWENTIETH-CENTURY BRITAIN
Kenneth O. Morgan
THE VIKINGS Julian Richards
WITTGENSTEIN A. C. Grayling
WORLD MUSIC Philip Bohlman
THE WORLD TRADE
ORGANIZATION Amrita Narlikar

Available soon:

1066 George Garnett
EXPRESSIONISM
Katerina Reed-Tsocha
GEOGRAPHY John A.Matthews and
David T. Herbert
HISTORY OF MEDICINE
William Bynum

MEMORY Jonathan Foster
NELSON MANDELA Elleke Boehmer
SCIENCE AND RELIGION
Thomas Dixon
SEXUALITY Véronique Mottier
THE MEANING OF LIFE
Terry Eagleton

For more information visit our website
www.oup.com/uk/vsi
www.oup.com/us

Nicholas Boyle

GERMAN LITERATURE

A Very Short Introduction

OXFORD
UNIVERSITY PRESS

OXFORD

UNIVERSITY PRESS

Great Clarendon Street, Oxford OX2 6DP

Oxford University Press is a department of the University of Oxford.
It furthers the University's objective of excellence in research, scholarship,
and education by publishing worldwide in

Oxford New York

Auckland Cape Town Dar es Salaam Hong Kong Karachi
Kuala Lumpur Madrid Melbourne Mexico City Nairobi
New Delhi Shanghai Taipei Toronto

With offices in

Argentina Austria Brazil Chile Czech Republic France Greece
Guatemala Hungary Italy Japan Poland Portugal Singapore
South Korea Switzerland Thailand Turkey Ukraine Vietnam

Oxford is a registered trade mark of Oxford University Press
in the UK and in certain other countries

Published in the United States
by Oxford University Press Inc., New York

British Library Cataloguing in Publication Data

Data available

Library of Congress Cataloging in Publication Data

Data available

ISBN 978–0–19–920659–9

1 3 5 7 9 10 8 6 4 2

Typeset by SPI Publisher Services, Pondicherry, India
Printed in Great Britain by
Ashford Colour Press Ltd, Gosport, Hampshire

Contents

Acknowledgements ix

List of illustrations xi

Introduction 1

1 The bourgeois and the official: a historical overview 5

2 The laying of the foundations (to 1781) 27

3 The age of idealism (1781–1832) 58

4 The age of materialism (1832–1914) 80

5 Traumas and memories (1914–) 120

Further reading 160

Index 163

Acknowledgements

I am grateful to students and colleagues in the Department of German in the University of Cambridge for their discussions of this project with me, and particularly to Chris Young for his advice about my account of the earlier period. Discussions with Raymond Geuss enabled me to understand Paul Celan better. I should also like to express my thanks to Andrea Keegan and her colleagues at Oxford University Press for their helpful and understanding treatment of a fond author in love with too bulky a manuscript. My wife, Rosemary, was, as usual, an indispensable support in what turned out be – again, as usual – a bigger undertaking than I originally imagined. I am especially grateful to Susan Few for her help in preparing the typescript.

The intellectual debts incurred in writing a book of this kind are many, and some of them of very long standing. I could not have conceived it without the inspiration and example of my teachers and I dedicate it therefore to Ronald Gray and the late Peter Stern.

List of illustrations

1 Map of Germany, 1871 to 1918 **3**

2 Wilhelm I proclaimed as German Emperor, Versailles, 1871 **16**
   bpk

3 Apostles, by Tilman Riemenschneider **29**
   akg-images

4 Luther as an Augustinian friar, 1520 **31**
   akg-images

5 Christoph Martin Wieland, 1806 **43**
   akg-images

6 August Wilhelm Iffland, in Schiller's *The Robbers* **56**
   akg-images

7 *A Glimpse of Greece at its Zenith* (1825), by Karl Friedrich Schinkel **69**
   bpk/Nationalgalerie SMB/ Jörg P. Anders

8 Life mask of Goethe (1807) **77**
   Deutsches Literatur-Archiv, Marbach

9 *The Poor Poet* (1839), by Carl Spitzweg **90**
   bpk/Nationalgalerie SMB/ Jörg P. Anders

10 Wilhelm Busch, scenes from *Hans Huckebein* (1867) **95**

11 Ludwig II's Wagnerian dream-world at Neuschwanstein, 1870s **99**
    akg-images

12 Nietzsche, with his friend, Paul Rée, and Lou Andreas-Salome **103**
    akg-images

13 Title of the first edition of *The Seventh Ring* (1907) by Stefan George **106**
    Stefan-George-Stiftung, Stuttgart

14 Emil Orlik, poster for *The Weavers*, 1897 **111**

15 Heinrich and Thomas Mann, 1927 **121**
© World History Archive/Topfoto

16 Bertolt Brecht, 1927 **127**
Mary Evans Picture Library/Interfoto

17 Martin Heidegger, 1933 **135**
akg-images

18 Paul Celan, 1967 **146**
akg-images/ullstein bild

19 *The Tin Drum*: Günter Grass, with David Bennent and Volker Schlöndorff, 1979 **153**
Picture-alliance/dpa/
© dpa-Bilderdienst

The publisher and the author apologize for any errors or omissions in the above list. If contacted they will be pleased to rectify these at the earliest opportunity.

Introduction

Literature is not just texts, because texts are not just texts. Texts are always turned, and turn their readers, to something other than texts and readers, something the texts are about. An introduction, even a very short introduction, to a national literature cannot be just an introduction to texts, it is also an introduction to a nation. To ask what German literature is like is to ask what – from a literary point of view – Germany is like. Since the foundation in the 18th century of the two distinctively modern literary genres, the book of subjective lyrical poems and the objective realistic novel, there have been two voices of literary modernity, and Germany has spoken, supremely, with one of them: poetic, tragic, resolutely reflective, and subliminally religious. The other voice – novelistic, realistic, sometimes comic, sometimes morally earnest – has in the German tradition been more muted, though by no means mute. This book is concerned with the character of Germany's literary contribution to our modern self-understanding, and so with the character of the community to and about which, and in whose language, its writers primarily expressed themselves. The first thing to say about that community is that, for all the centrality of Germany in European geography, history, and culture, it is not unified, and never has been.

From a British point of view, 'Central Europe' probably means somewhere unreliable north of Transylvania. But *'Mitteleuropa'*

('Central Europe') is how contemporary Germans describe the area in which they live, and with justification. Since the fall of Rome, Europe's trade routes from North to South and East to West have intersected on German territory. Forms of the modern German language have been spoken from the Rhine to the Volga and from the borders of Finland to the southern slopes of the Italian Alps. Language, culture, and genes have been exchanged, over the centuries, in peace and war, with French, Italian, Hungarian, Slavonic, and Scandinavian neighbours. (In addition to Germany, Austria, and Switzerland, German is an official language in part or all of Belgium, Hungary, Italy, Liechtenstein, Luxembourg, Namibia, and Poland.) Lacking clear geographical boundaries, however, Germany has been a point of reference for the European identities grouped around it without establishing an identity of its own. The speakers of German have never been united in a single state calling itself Germany, not even by Hitler. The modern state of that name is one, historically unique, result of a long and complex development. The process which brought together the Federal and Democratic Republics in 1990–1 was known as 're-unification' but the state that emerged from it has different boundaries from any of its predecessors and a significant proportion of its older population was born outside it, though in territories that had thought of themselves as German, in some cases, for many centuries. Europe's other two principal German-speaking states, Austria and Switzerland, have had rather more continuity of identity, even if Austria, as the former metropolitan state of an empire which lasted under various names from 1526 to 1918, has reached its present equilibrium only through the trauma of multiple amputation. German-speaking Switzerland (though each canton has its own history) has developed independently of the other German lands since the 15th century, if not before.

What is called German literature is really three separate literatures, of three separate states, as distinct as the literatures of, say, England, America, and Australia. Dürrenmatt was no more

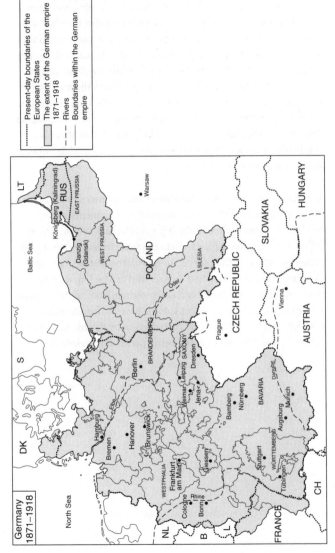

Germany	Present-day boundaries of the
1871–1918	European States
	The extent of the German empire 1871–1918
	Rivers
	Boundaries within the German empire

LT

RUS

Baltic Sea

EAST PRUSSIA

Königsberg (Kaliningrad)

Danzig (Gdańsk)

WEST PRUSSIA

Warsaw

POLAND

BRANDENBURG

Oder

SILESIA

S

Berlin

CZECH REPUBLIC

Prague

DK

North Sea

Hamburg

Elbe

Bremen

Hanover

Brunswick

Leipzig

Weimar

Dresden

SAXONY

Jena

Bamberg

Nürnberg

BAVARIA

Danube

SLOVAKIA

AUSTRIA

Vienna

HUNGARY

NL

WESTPHALIA

Frankfurt am Main

Giessen

Cologne

Rhine

Bonn

B

L

Stuttgart

Augsburg

Munich

WÜRTTEMBERG

Tübingen

CH

FRANCE

1. Germany at its greatest extent, between 1871 and 1918

a German writer because his plays were put on in Berlin than Arthur Miller was an English writer because his plays were put on in London, and to call Kafka a German novelist is rather like calling Seamus Heaney a British poet: there is some truth in the phrase, but only because it points to a tension between the writer's origins and material, on the one hand, and his medium and his public, on the other. This book is concerned with the literature of the state now called Germany, which needs to be seen in isolation from the literatures of Austria and Switzerland if its own peculiar dynamic is to become visible. Rambling though it is, there is a single tale to tell and it cannot be told outside its specific political, social, and even economic setting.

In order to bring out the coherence of the German story, I begin with a synopsis of political and cultural developments since the Middle Ages, without referring to individual writers. There follow four chapters which keep to the same framework but give rather more detail. Chapters dealing with the Middle Ages and the literatures of Austria and Switzerland can be found on the internet (http://www.mml.can.ac.uk/german/staff/nb215). Those who miss Kafka in the present volume have the benefit of the excellent *Kafka: A Very Short Introduction* by Ritchie Robertson (OUP, 2004), Chapters 1 and 4 being particularly relevant.

Chapter 1
The bourgeois and the official: a historical overview

German literature, in the narrow sense, is the literature of the states, predominantly the Lutheran states, of the Holy Roman Empire, and of their 19th-century successor kingdoms, which were gathered by Bismarck into his Second Empire and, after an interval as the Weimar Republic, formed the core of Hitler's Third Empire. Austria, though a part of the Holy Roman Empire, can be excluded from this story, as Bismarck excluded it, together with Hungary and Austria's other, non-Imperial, territories in the Danube basin. Prussia, however, has to be included because of its crucial role in the political definition of Germany, even though the duchy, later kingdom, of Prussia (now divided between Poland, the Baltic states, and Russia) was never part of the Empire but was an external power-base for the Electors of Brandenburg, rather like Austria's Danubian hinterland, and even though Brandenburg-Prussia contributed little of significance to German literature, outside the realm of philosophy, until the 19th century.

The clergy and the university

The Lutheranism is important. The Reformation of the early 16th century marks the beginning of German literature, in the sense of the term used here. Not just because the Reformation followed relatively soon (and doubtless not by chance) on the linguistic changes which brought into existence the modern form of the German language, and on the invention of moveable-type printing, which made it desirable, and feasible, to have a standard written language for the whole area across which German books might circulate. By transferring the responsibility for the defence of the Christian faith from the Emperor to the local princes, the Reformation made it possible to imagine a German (Protestant) cultural identity that could do without the Empire altogether, as free of political links to the Roman past as it was of religious links to the Roman present. More, the Reformation launched the individual Protestant states on a voyage towards cultural and political self-sufficiency even within the German-speaking world. In particular their clergy, then the largest class of the professionally educated and professionally literate, the bearers of cultural values and memory, were cut off from their fellows, even their fellow Protestants, by the boundaries of their state and their historical epoch. They could call only with reservations on the experience of Christians in other places and times and, in practical matters, they had to make their careers in dependence, direct or indirect, on the local monarch. Charged with providing, or supervising, primary education and other charitable activities, such as the care of orphans, which in Catholic states remained the responsibility of relatively independent religious orders or local religious houses, Protestant ministers were often virtually an executive branch of the state civil service.

The instrumentalization of the clergy in the Protestant princely states exercised a profound influence on German literature and philosophy because of a peculiarity in Germany's political and economic development. The towns, mainly Imperial Free Cities, which in the late Middle Ages had been the most dynamic element in German society – centres of commerce, industry, and banking which were also the centres of a richly inventive middle-class culture, especially in the visual arts – went into decline in the century after the Reformation and failed to adjust to Europe's shift from overland to overseas trade and to the new importance of the maritime nations. Germany's devastating religious civil war, the Thirty Years War from 1618 to 1648, sealed their fate. In the post-war period only the state powers could raise the capital necessary for reconstruction, and with few exceptions, the great Free Cities decayed into mere 'home towns'. The princely territories, with their predominantly agricultural economies and rural populations that could be pressed into military service, gained correspondingly in relative power and influence. A political revolt of the middle classes, which in 16th-century Holland and 17th-century England was largely successful but which in France went underground with the suppression of the Fronde by the young Louis XIV, was in Germany out of the question. The Empire became a federation of increasingly absolute monarchs who in cultural as in political matters looked to the France of the Sun King as their model. The courtly arts, such as architecture and opera, dedicated to the entertainment and glorification of the prince and his entourage, did well, but printed books were predominantly academic (so often in Latin) or, if they were intended to circulate more widely among the depressed middle classes, were either trivial fantasies, without social or political significance, or works of religious devotion commending contentment with one's lot. One institution, however, of the greatest importance to the middle class, which after the middle of the 17th century flourished better in Germany than elsewhere in Europe, was the university. At a time when England made do with two universities, Germany, with only four or five times the population, had around 40. The university had come late to the German lands – the first was at Prague in 1348 – but in the post-Reformation world it had a quite new significance. The absolute, princely state, with its ambition to control everything, needed officers to carry its will into every part of its domains, and these the university provided, principally, until the later 18th century, by training the clergy. Practical subjects, such as finance and agriculture, were also taught, and much earlier in Germany than in England, but always with a view to their utility in the state administration. The offspring of well-to-do professionals could afford to study law and medicine and rely on family connections to find them a billet, but for an able young man from a poor background the theology faculty, much the largest and most richly endowed, offered the best prospects of social advancement and future employment.

The 18th-century crisis

Eighteenth-century Germany was a stagnant society in which economic and political power was largely concentrated in the hands of the state, and intellectual life was initially in the grip of the state churches. There was little room for private enterprise, material or cultural. Yet this society experienced a literary and philosophical explosion, the consequences of which are still with us. The constriction itself put up the boiler pressure. In England and France there was a significant property-owning middle class, a bourgeoisie in the full sense of the word, able to find an outlet for its capital and its energies in trade and industry, emigration and empire, and eventually in political revolution and reform. In Germany the equivalent class was proportionally much smaller and shut away in the towns, where it could engage in political or economic activity of only local importance. What Germany had in abundance was a class of state officials (and of Protestant clergymen who were state officials by another name), who were close to political power, and were often its executive arm, but who could not exercise it in their own right, and could only look on enviously at the achievements of their counterparts in England, Holland, or Switzerland, or, after 1789, in France: 'They do the deeds, and we translate the narrations of them into German', wrote one of them. The only outlet for the energies of this peculiarly German middle class was the book. Germany in the 18th century had more writers per head than anywhere else in Europe, roughly one for every 5,000 of the entire population. Its first industrial capitalists, its only private entrepreneurs who before 1800 were mass-producing goods for a mass market, were its publishers. In the middle of the 18th century Germany's official class entered a crisis. The Seven Years War (1756–63) definitively established Prussia as the dominant Protestant power in the Empire and, on the continent of Europe, a counterweight to Catholic Austria, while Prussia's ally, England, emerged similarly victorious on the world stage in the race for colonies at the expense of its Catholic rival, France. Yet at this moment when – at least from a German point of view – Anglo-German Protestantism seemed to have demonstrated its superiority in all respects over Europe's Catholic South, the religious heart of the cultural alliance began to succumb to an enemy within. Under the name of Enlightenment, the deist and historicist critique of Christianity, which had originated largely in England, began to detach Germany's theologically educated elite from the faith of their fathers. Since there was not much of a private sector in which an ex-cleric could seek alternative employment, and since loyalty to the state church was something of a touchstone for loyalty to the state itself, a crisis of conscience was an existential crisis too. The struggle for a way out was a matter of intellectual and sometimes personal life and death. Two generations of unprecedented mental exertion and suffering within the pressure-vessel of the German state brought into existence some of the most characteristic features of modern culture, which elsewhere took much longer to develop.

Two routes led out of the crisis, one considerably more secure than the other. First, it was possible to adapt Germany's most distinctive state institution, the university, to meet the new need. New career paths, inside and outside academic life, became available for those with a scholarly bent but a distaste for theology, through the creation of new subjects of study or the expansion of previously minor options. Classical philology, modern history, languages and literatures, the history of art, the natural sciences, education itself, and, perhaps most influential of all, idealist philosophy – in these new or newly significant university disciplines 18th and early 19th-century Germany established a pre-eminence which, in some cases, has lasted into the present. Second, and more precariously, the ex-theologian could turn to the one area of private enterprise and commercial activity readily accessible to him: the book market. It has been calculated that, even excluding philosophers, 120 major literary figures writing in German and born between 1676 and 1804 had either studied theology or were the children of Protestant pastors. But there was a snare concealed behind the lure of literature. To make money a book had to circulate widely among the middle classes, the professionals and business people, and their wives and daughters, not just among the officials. But these were the classes that the political constitution of absolutist Germany excluded from power and influence. It was not therefore possible to write about the real forces shaping German life and at the same time to write about something familiar and important to a wide readership. The price of success was triviality and falsification; if you were seriously devoted to real issues you would stay esoteric, and poor. The German literary revival of the 18th century was in great measure the attempt, fuelled by secularization, to resolve this dilemma. Especially in the earlier phases it seemed that the example of England, the ally in Protestantism, might be the answer, and hopes of a German equivalent to the English realistic novel, at once truthful and popular, ran high. But Germany could not model its literature on that of England's self-confident and largely self-governing capitalist middle class. Its social and economic starting point was different, and it had to find its own way.

In Germany, political power and cultural influence were concentrated in absolute rulers and their immediate entourage, loosely termed the 'courts'. The interface between these centres and the rest of society, and specifically the groups that made up the reading public, was provided by the state officials. Therefore, the class of officials – those who belonged to it, those who were educated for it, and those who sought access to it – formed the growth zone for the German national literature. In material terms, a state salary, whether a cleric's, a professor's, or an administrator's, or even just a personal pension from the monarch, provided a foundation so that a literary career, albeit part-time, was at least possible and did not have to be a relentless chase after maximal earnings. In intellectual terms, the writers' proximity to power, and to the state institutions, meant that the issues they raised in the symbolic medium of literature were genuinely central to the national life and identity, even if their perspective was that of non-participants. The public literary genre which most precisely reflected the ambiguous realities of life in the growth zone, and which, towards the end of the century, reached a point of perfection subsequently recognized as 'classical', was the poetic drama, the drama which, though performable and performed, was most widely distributed and appreciated as a printed book. The dramatic form reflected the political and cultural dominance of the princely court, for none of Germany's many theatres were purely commercial undertakings, all required some kind of state subsidy, and even in the Revolutionary period most still served their original and principal function of entertaining the ruler. Circulation as a book, however, as Germany's equivalent of a novel, both truthful and commercially successful, reflected the aspiration of the middle classes to a market-based culture of their own. And, finally, the philosophical, if not explicitly theological, tenor of the themes of these plays reflected the secularization of Lutheranism which was providing a new vocabulary for the description of personal and social existence, whether by playwrights in the state theatres or by professors in the state universities. Among the most important elements in this new vocabulary were the concepts of moral (rather than political) 'freedom' and of 'Art', as the realm of human experience in which this freedom was made visible. The German 'classical' era gave to the world not only the meaning of the word 'Art' which enabled Oscar Wilde to say nearly a hundred years later that it was quite useless, but also the belief that literature was primarily 'Art' (rather than, say, a means of communication).

The rise of bourgeois Germany

'Germany' around 1800 was not so much a geographical as a literary expression. The most powerful impetus to give it a political meaning probably came from Napoleon. He imposed the abolition of the ecclesiastical territories, a radical reduction in the number of the principalities from over 300 to about 40, and the organization of the remainder into a federation of sovereign states, even before the formal dissolution of the Holy Roman Empire in 1806. His annihilating defeat of Prussia in the same year forced on it a programme of modernization which was to determine German social and political structures for the next century and a half. The modernization did not, however, take the republican form it had taken in France, and though constitutionalism briefly flourished when it was necessary to rouse the people to throw off the Napoleonic yoke from the necks of their princes, it was abandoned after the Carlsbad Decrees of 1819 which turned Germany, until 1848, into a confederation of police states. The Prussian commercial, industrial, and professional middle classes were still too weak to challenge the king, or even the landowning nobility (the *Junkers*), and introduce representative government or a separation of legislature and executive. Instead the successful bid for power came from the king's officials, and the autocratic absolutism of the 18th century gave way to the bureaucratic absolutism of the 19th – a rule of law, free of conscious corruption and directed to the common welfare, but imposing a military level of discipline on all layers of society. The king's personal decisions remained final, but they were increasingly mediated, and so to some extent checked, by his civil and armed services, into which the nobility were gradually absorbed – partly as a brake on the ambitions of the middle class. The new Prussia, the largest and most powerful of the German Protestant states, had an altogether new significance for its fellows, once the old Imperial framework had vanished. Territories which before 1806 could pass as constituent parts of a larger whole, however ramshackle and loosely defined, now had to justify themselves as economically and politically self-sufficient states, a task to which none of them, apart from Prussia, Austria, and perhaps Bavaria, could pretend to be equal. Some kind of association between them had to be found. There was a supine intergovernmental 'Federation' dominated by Austria and a much more effective Customs Union (*Zollverein*) of a smaller number of territories grouped round Prussia, but the word 'Germany' now meant something future and unreal. If it had once referred to the Empire and any other territories attached to the Empire in which German was spoken and written, now it meant the political unit in which all, or most, German-speakers would find their home. And there was the rub: who precisely was to be included in this future Germany? It could hardly contain both Prussia and Austria, as the old Empire and the new Federation were able, more or less, to contain them – though there were many dreamers to whom this seemed possible, among them the author of '*Deutschland, Deutschland über alles*' – but equally it could hardly exclude them, given their influence over the smaller states and frequent interventions in their affairs. In practice, the two great powers were resolving the issue for themselves: Prussia was expanding purposefully westwards to the Rhineland, while Austria was withdrawing from German affairs to concentrate on its non-German-speaking territories in Eastern Europe and North Italy. In the end, the Protestant intellectuals of Northern Germany, still held together, as under the old regime, by the publishing industry and the university network, threw in their lot with Prussia. After a decade of increasing agitation, 1848, Europe's 'year of revolutions', saw the summoning of the Frankfurt Parliament, a quarter of whose membership was made up of academics, clergy, and writers, and which in 1849 offered the Prussian monarch the kingship of a Germany without Austria. Friedrich Wilhelm IV refused to rule by the free choice of his subjects – 'to pick up a crown from the gutter' – though his brother, Wilhelm I, accepted the same 'lesser German' (*kleindeutsch*) crown when Bismarck secured it for him by force of arms in 1866–71.

To the extent to which it was a revolution of professors, and perhaps rather further, the failed German revolution of 1848 was a revolution of the officials, the last act, and the finest hour, of the 18th-century reading public. It was an attempt to unify Germany by constitutional and administrative means, while retaining for government, and monarchical government at that, the leading role in the structuring of society. But the balance of power in the German middle class was already beginning to shift fundamentally. Between 1815 and 1848 the population grew by 60%, and as poverty intensified the need for employment grew desperate. After some tentative, state-sponsored beginnings in the 1830s, a first wave of industrialization was felt in the 1840s, with huge (often foreign) investments in a railway network, mainly within the Customs Union, and a consequent economic upswing. The decade ended with an economic as well as a political crash, and with the last of the pre-industrial famines (partly caused by the same potato blight that devastated Ireland) – factors that together led (as in Ireland) to a surge in emigration. But in the following 20 years Prussia, governed from 1862 by Bismarck, embraced economic liberalism as a means of sweeping away historic and institutional obstacles to the unification of its heterogeneous territories, and the long period of intensive growth began which was to transform Germany into an industrial giant. As a result, when the Second German Empire was founded in 1871 it had a bourgeoisie, a property-owning and money-making class, which was much larger, wealthier, and more significant for the common good than anything the First Empire had known. The consequences for literature and philosophy were far-reaching. As this class emerged, it battled for self-respect and cultural identity with the long-established middle-class instruments of state power, the officials. The revived bourgeoisie had a more obvious interest in the economic and political unification of Germany than civil servants who owed their positions to the multiplication of power centres, and entry to it was not dependent on passage through the universities. In the early years of the 19th century its frustrated political ambitions expressed themselves, particularly in Prussia, in the literature of escape known as 'Romanticism', but as it gained in confidence its literary culture took on a more explicitly revolutionary, anti-official colour – though the oppositional stance betrayed a continuing dependence on what was being opposed. After the humiliation of official Germany at Frankfurt, however, with industry and commerce flourishing in the sunshine of state approval, any sense of inferiority passed, the icons of the previous century were cheerfully ridiculed, literature itself became a paying concern as copyright became enforceable, and novels and plays with such strictly bourgeois themes as money, materialism, and social justice emerged from the realm of the trivial and, for a while, linked Germany's written culture with that of its neighbours in Western Europe. The uniquely – for the outside world perhaps impenetrably – German culture of the late 18th-century Golden Age, scholarly, humanist, cosmopolitan, survived under the patronage of the lesser courts, in the lee of political events and economic changes, until 1848, but thereafter it declined into academicism or, in the case of the kings of Bavaria, into eccentricity. But though the official class had lost supremacy, it had not lost power, and through the universities, despite the growth of private cultural societies and foundations, it remained the guardian of the national past. As the redefinition of the German state came to preoccupy all minds, so the servants of the state were able to retain for themselves a certain authority and the two main factions in the middle class sank their differences in the national interest. The concept of '*Bildung*', meaning both 'culture' and 'education', was the ideological medium in which this fusion could take place, the value on which all could agree, precisely because it left carefully ambiguous whether you achieved '*Bildung*' by going to university or simply by reading, or at any rate approving, the right books. The term '*Bildungsbürger*' gained a currency at this time which it has never since lost. Suggesting a middle class united by its experience of '*Bildung*', its main function is to identify the official with the bourgeois, to create a community of interest between salaried servants of the state and tradesmen, property owners, and

2. The proclamation of Wilhelm I as German Emperor, 1 January 1871, in the Hall of Mirrors, Versailles (Anton von Werner, 1885). Bismarck is in the centre. The treaty of Versailles was signed in the same room in 1919 at the end of Germany's Second Empire

self-employed professionals. A crucial step in the definition of '*Bildung*' was the canonizing of the literary achievements of the official class as 'classical'. Germany in 1871 was not only to be a nation like England or France – it was to have its literary classics like them too.

In Bismarck's new Germany the bourgeoisie was accommodated, but kept on a short lead. It was given a voice in the Reichstag, the Imperial Diet, and the lesser representative assemblies of the constituent states, but the executive, with the Imperial Chancellor at its head, was in no formal way responsible to these parliaments. In practice, of course, the Chancellor needed their co-operation to secure his legislative programme and so officialdom lost the almost absolute power it had enjoyed in the earlier part of the century. But the dominant model for a society in which military service was compulsory was provided by the army (with the upper ranks reserved for the nobility), and Bismarck and his successors treated all attempts to establish parliamentary accountability as insubordination: the socialist party was virtually proscribed for over a decade. Within the constraints imposed by the supreme priority of national unity, the agents of autocracy continued to look down on those they regarded as self-interested individualists and materialists because they made money for themselves, rather than receiving a salary from the state. In the world of '*Bildung*' too the profession of a shared devotion to the national tradition papered over the deep animosity between those who wrote for a living and the university intellectuals whose literary activity was now largely confined to historical and critical study. Like Bismarck, the professor of 'Germanistics' – as it was beginning to be called – had as little taste for the bourgeois as for the socialists, Catholics, Jews, or women who were now unfortunately as likely as the bourgeois to involve themselves in the national literature.

In the turmoil of 1848–9, a little-noticed pamphlet, drafted by a German philosopher for a tiny group of English radicals, and with the title of *The Communist Manifesto*, had prophesied that the free markets aspired to by the national bourgeoisies would grow into a global market, a '*Weltmarkt*'. By the 1870s that prophecy was clearly coming true. Germany's first experience of globalization was painful, however. The worldwide stock-market crash of 1873, which began in Vienna, led to a long depression from which the world did not emerge until the 1890s. In Germany the depression was relatively shallow and some growth continued, though in the 1880s net emigration (which had totalled 3 million over the previous four decades) reached an all-time high of 1.3 million – a figure which is itself a measure of the intensity of globalization. In 1879 Bismarck was moved by the effect of cheap American grain imports on the incomes of the land-owning *Junkers* to listen to the growing demands for protection from other quarters as well, particularly the heavy industry that would be of strategic importance in wartime, and to abandon his earlier policy of free trade, erecting a tariff wall round his new state. At the same time, he put an end to his 'cultural war' (*Kulturkampf*) with the Catholic Church and endeavoured to outflank the working-class movement by introducing Europe's first system of social security. His motives in establishing 'state socialism', as it was soon called, were no different from those that had guided him earlier, and which had deep roots in the German past: first, the overriding need for unity in the state and, second, the interests of the agricultural nobility which continued to furnish Prussia with its ruling class. But the protectionist course on which Germany and the other European states now embarked, and which was eventually adopted even by Britain, long the staunchest advocate, and greatest beneficiary, of free trade, accentuated the division of Europe, and the world, into would-be autarkic blocs. Thanks to the inability of politicians, of any country, to imagine an international institutional order which would accommodate to each other the competing energies of numerous growing economies, the developed states, whether empires, federations, or unitary nations, set out to achieve economic and political – that is, military – self-sufficiency. Germany's bid for colonies in Africa and the South Seas, which began in 1884, was not so much a serious geopolitical move as a symbolic irritant. Like the huge expansion of the navy, it was a declaration that Germany was anyone's equal and could look after itself. As general growth resumed in the 1890s it became clear that, with its armed forces backed by the largest chemical and electrical industries in the world, and a coal and steel industry that was catching up on the British, Germany was capable, not necessarily of displacing the British Empire, but certainly of disputing its power to impose its own will. A British hegemony was giving way to a bi-polar world, and from the turn of the century something like a Cold War began in the cultural sphere. Britain turned away from the German models, particularly in philosophy and scholarship, which had had great prestige since the days of the Prince Consort, while voices in Germany emphasized the uniqueness of German literary, musical, and philosophical achievements and the need to protect 'Kultur' (the creation of the official classes) from contamination by the materialistic and journalistic (that is, bourgeois) 'civilization' of the West. The fusion of disparate elements in the concept of the '*Bildungsbürger*', though rejected by some of the most clear-sighted critics of the Second Empire, was sustained by projecting its tensions outwards on to the relations between nations and defining a unique role for the new Germany. Britain and France at this time wove similar myths of their own special mission in world-history. Tariff walls became walls in the mind, and the mental effects were as serious as the economic distortions which put increasing strains on the inadequate international political order. After more than a decade of toying by the nations of Europe with fantasies of their own exceptionality, in 1914 the war-games went real.

The officials strike back

Globalization spelled the end of the bourgeoisie, in the strict sense, and not only in Germany. A class living solely off its capital, off the alienated labour of others, was sustainable only by societies with open frontiers, with open spaces into which the disadvantaged and disaffected could expand. As the world economy grew into a single closed system, and as societies that shrank from the challenge of the political co-operation required by economic integration sought – in vain, of course – to seal themselves off in smaller units, so there was less and less room for a leisured capitalist class, and it was forced increasingly into work. The intrusion of work into the world of capital was reflected, in the first decades of the 20th century, in an intellectual upheaval which broke apart the forms and conventions of the earlier stages of cultural modernity and was at least as violent in Germany and Austria as anywhere else. In literature, art, music, philosophy, and psychology, the concepts of identity, collective and personal, that had been appropriate to an age when the world was wide, and economic expansion was untrammelled by political institutions, were subjected to intense and hostile scrutiny. It was Germany's misfortune that the representatives of the bourgeoisie achieved the political autonomy, and even supremacy, for which they had been struggling for well over half a century, only when their social and economic and even their cultural position was fatally undermined. In 1918 Germany had its revolution at last. But the new republic was born in military defeat and shackled at once by an unequal peace. It was shorn, not only of its symbolic overseas empire, but of much of its mineral wealth in the territories returned to France and the resurrected Poland. Its middle class, which had grown into prosperity over the previous two generations, was pauperized in the terrible inflations which reflected the lack of confidence in its future, and, with the loss of their capital, many private foundations and charities, old and new, ceased to exist. Its rivals, cushioned for a while yet by empire, and by the complacency of victory, could afford to ignore the challenge to their identity implicit in the global market. But Germany and Austria, friendless and unsupported by the labour of subject peoples, had to make their way back to prosperity by their own efforts, as the world's first post-imperial, and post-bourgeois, nations. The culture of the German and Austrian successor-states in the age of the Weimar Republic had about it a radical modernity, indeed postmodernity, whose full relevance to the condition of the rest of the world became apparent only after 1989.

In one crucial respect, however, the Weimar Republic had not been released from its past. The German bourgeoisie might have been reduced to a few super-rich families heading the vertically integrated industrial and banking cartels that had prospered in the days of Bismarck's 'state socialism'. But the other component of the middle class, the officials (including the professorate), had survived the debacle remarkably unscathed. The authoritarian monarch had gone, but the state apparatus remained, and its instinct was either to serve authority, or to embody it. The army, the academy, and the administration hankered after their king. They were ill at ease with parliamentary institutions that bestowed the authority of the state on a proletarianized mass society – that is, a society based not on the ownership of land, or even of capital, but on the need and obligation to work. The representative bodies of the Second Empire, crudely divided between nationalists and socialists, had been, largely, a sham and, once the monarchy that was the reason for their existence had passed away, they could not be grown on as a native democratic tradition. Nor was there any obvious external source of democratic inspiration. For nationalists there was no reason to look kindly on the liberal traditions of the victor powers, who hypocritically imposed self-determination on Poles and Czechs, in order to break up Germany and Austria, but withheld it from Indians and Africans, in order to preserve their own empires. To socialists it seemed more important that communist Russia had correctly identified the proletarian nature of modern society than that it was maintaining and extending the brutal Tsarist regime of social discipline. In the absence of native republican models, and with the Prussian inheritance still obscuring the view back to the Holy Roman Empire, the continuing identity of 'Germany' was largely guaranteed by the persistence of the official class and its ideology of apolitical '*Bildung*'. The ideology, however, diverted all but the most perceptive writers from the task of defending the constitution. On the one hand, any number of new theories of 'art' provided as many reasons for dismissing contemporary politics as superficial or inauthentic. On the other, the acceptance of political engagement could lead to a general rejection of conventional 'culture' and a coarse anti-intellectualism. The Weimar Republic was betrayed on all sides, and if the writers and artists, on the whole, betrayed it from the left, the public service, including the professors, betrayed it, massively and effectively, from the right. The National Socialist German Workers' Party presented itself, like 'state socialism', as above the distinction between left and right, as the party of national unity in the new age of work, but its appeal was unambiguously that of nostalgia for the authoritarianism decapitated in 1918. Its opportunity came when the excitement of global recovery in the 1920s faltered and, after the great crash of 1929, gave way to global depression. The disastrous decision of the Western nations to respond to this crisis with protectionism took in Germany in 1933 the form of electing a government committed to withdrawing the country from all international institutions and establishing in the economy, as in the whole of society, a command structure based on a military model – a queerly deranged memory of the Second Empire. In the Third Empire, however, there was none of Bismarck's subtle accommodation with bourgeois free enterprise. It was the period of officialdom's greatest and most cancerous expansion, as new layers of uniformed bureaucrats were imposed on old in a permanent revolution generating permanent turf wars, and all the while new, malign, and irrational policies were executed with the same humdrum efficiency or inefficiency as ever and the traditions of Frederick the Great and the 19th-century reformers terminated in Eichmann and the camp commandants who played Schubert at the end of a day's work. By this stage, however, the culture of the German official class had ceased to be productive and was almost entirely passive. The universities, emptied of anyone of independent mind or Jewish descent, lost their global pre-eminence for ever. The agitprop generated by the 'Ministry of Popular Enlightenment' in the form of films, pulp fiction, or public art is of interest now only to the historical sociologist. Music and the performing arts were parasitic on the achievements of the past, which by and large they caricatured. The free and creative literary spirits, whether or not they had had official positions, were nearly all either dead or in an exile which they found very difficult to relate to their experience of Germany's past or its present. The professors of philosophy and 'Germanistics' who stayed behind devoted themselves at best to relatively harmless editorial projects. Of the worst it is still impossible to speak with moderation.

After zero hour

After 1871, 1918, and 1933, the fourth redefinition of Germany within a lifetime began in 1945. Territorially the adjustment was the biggest there had ever been. Millions moved westwards from areas that had had majority German populations for centuries. The state of Prussia was formally dissolved. Germany was returned approximately to the boundaries of the Holy Roman Empire (without Austria) at the time of the Reformation. Socially and politically too the zones occupied by Britain, France, and the USA recovered something of 16th-century Germany, before the rise of absolutism: a federal republic, with a Catholic majority, dominated by the industrial, commercial, and financial power of several great towns. Hitler had succeeded where all previous German revolutionaries had failed: he had made Germany into a classless society. For 12 years inherited wealth and station had counted for nothing; what mattered was race, party membership, and military rank. After the destruction, and self-destruction, of his absolutist regime the West German Bonn Republic began from a base of social equality unprecedented in the nation's history. But the foundation had been laid by Hitler's 'party of the workers' and thanks to the relatively rapid withdrawal of the occupying powers in the West the Federal Republic had from an early stage to confront, from its own resources, the question posed by its continuity with the immediate German past. At first the confrontation, in the public mind, took the form of a creative denial, the energetic construction of an alternative Germany, west-facing, republican, committed to free markets and European integration, and in economic terms highly successful. Culturally, however, the underlying continuity betrayed itself in a troubled relationship with the remoter past of the nation. The literary and philosophical achievements of the period around 1800 still enjoyed their Second Empire status of 'classics', but they were stylized and reinterpreted as an 'other Germany' of the mind from which, in some mysterious and fateful process, the Germany of 1871–1945 had become detached. To claim, however, that the Federal Republic had recovered that 'other Germany' – and the claim was implicit in the decision to call its cultural missions 'Goethe Institutes' – was to make the improbable claim that it somehow reincarnated the world of the late 18th-century principalities. The local German dialectic between bourgeois and official which created the literary culture of that era was at an end. The relentless advance of the global market had destroyed both parties: the European bourgeoisie was no more, swallowed up in the tide of proletarianization which has turned us all into consumer-producers for the mass market; officialdom had lost its privileged relationship to the national identity with the decline in significance of the nation-state and of the local centre of political power. Both the re-canonization of the classics and the contestation of their authority by critics who felt themselves sufficiently unimplicated in the German past to sit in judgement on it were failures to assess realistically the historical process in which the 18th-century literary revival, the rise and fall of German nationalism, and the emergence of the new republican Germany were all equally involved. The Russian zone of occupation, from 1949 the German Democratic Republic, was the site of unrealism's last stand. Here, as elsewhere behind the Wall – surely the ultimate tariff barrier – officialdom for 40 years enjoyed an Indian summer, in seamless real continuity with the previous regime of malignant bureaucracy but in total mental and emotional denial of any resemblance to it. Eastern Germany, in physical possession of many of the cultural storehouses of Bismarck's Prussia-centred Empire, claimed to be the only true inheritor of what the Second Empire had defined as 'classical' – though it implausibly represented the 'other Germany' as a great materialist tradition culminating in Marx, Engels, and the Socialist Unity Party. With some vacillations, which recall similar uncertainties in Hitler's cultural policy, this party line was maintained in theatres, museums, and the educational system. With far greater rigour than in the West, therefore, any interrogation of the present which threatened to reveal its affinities with the Germany of 1933–45 was suppressed, and the appalling crimes of that period were dismissed as somebody else's affair.

So it was left at first to relatively isolated writers and thinkers in the Federal Republic to begin defining an identity for the new Germany by remembering the nightmares from which it had awoken. Official memory, in what was left of the university system, struggled, on the whole unsuccessfully, to recover the literature of the previous two centuries as a living tradition. But poets and novelists and writers for radio, supported by a market eager for books, turned, with rather more effect, to the even more intractable task of relating private consciousness to the world-historical disasters that Germany had both inflicted and suffered, and gradually gained recognition outside Germany too. As the emigrant generation of the 1930s reached maturity, and as universities on either side of the Atlantic came to exchange personnel more freely, it also came to be appreciated in the wider world that German philosophy and critical theory still provided essential instruments for understanding the revolutionary changes of the 20th century, especially if they were allowed to interact with ideas from the English-speaking cultures. After 1968 some of these international developments accelerated, partly as a result of intensive French engagement with German thinkers, but Germany itself found it more difficult to move forward, perhaps because the rewards of a generation's reconstructive efforts were at last being enjoyed. The universities, transformed into institutions of mass education, finally lost their privileged position in the nation's intellectual life except perhaps in the area in which they had begun, Protestant theology. An affluent social security system took the sting of practical urgency out of domestic moral and political issues, whatever theoretical heat they generated. Above all, the gravitational field of the Democratic Republic pulled all left-wing thinking out of true, creating the illusion of a political alternative even when the regime was universally acknowledged to have lost all credit, spuriously reviving the attractions of ideas obsolete since 1918, such as authoritarian state socialism and German isolationism, and obscuring the significance of the once more rising tide of globalization. It was to the global 'culture industry', to an American TV series of 1979, not to 30 years of work by her native intelligentsia, that Germany owed her public awakening to the hideous truth that only then became generally known by the name of the 'Holocaust'. When the global market finally swept away the last vestige of old Germany in 1989–90, the redefinition of the nation – again the fourth in a lifetime – continued to be hampered by a persisting nostalgia which was only superficially directed at the old East (*Ostalgie*). In reality, it was the last – let us hope, fading – trace of an animosity that runs through 250 years of German literary engagement with the concept of nationhood: the animosity between the official and the bourgeois, between the representatives of state power (which makes people virtuous) and the forces that make money (and so make people happy). In the '*Weltmarkt*', the conflict between the economic system and political power has certainly not gone away – if anything, it has intensified – but it is more diffused, at once more intangibly collective and more internal to the individual. For nearly three centuries the German literary and philosophical tradition has been compelled by local circumstances to concentrate on the point where the opposing forces collide. But there has always also been a cosmopolitan, or internationalist, vein in German literature, and those who in recent generations have tapped into it – even perhaps at the cost of a life of wandering or exile – have been more able than strictly national writers to make Germany's traumas into symbols of general significance for other countries caught like their own between a national past and a global future.

Chapter 2
The laying of the foundations (to 1781)

(i) Towns and princes (to 1720)

From the middle of the 13th century, the social and political tensions were becoming apparent that were to determine the culture of modern Germany. A decline in the authority of the Holy Roman Emperors coincided with a European population explosion and an economic boom. Although plague and a worsening climate halted the continental expansion in the later 14th century, Germany by then had several major urban centres, notably Cologne, Augsburg, and later Nuremberg, with around 50,000 inhabitants, which were comparable to contemporary London. The modern commercial and banking system, born in Italy around 1200, of which the German cities were soon a part, brought with it new political and cultural attitudes. The cities which, in a long struggle with Germany's lesser rulers, the Emperors had freed from princely overlordship were, like the Italian city-states, oligarchic rather than democratic in any modern sense, but they were self-governing, through elective councils, and once the guilds, representing industry, had won a place alongside the merchants and bankers, political and economic life were closely integrated. Military and feudal values, such as obedience and honour, were overshadowed by values derived from the economic process, such as productivity and enjoyment, and by an interest in the spiritual significance of the material world. Above all, the monetarization of economic relations, the replacement of feudal dues and payments in kind by rents paid in cash, a process which in urban areas was largely complete by the end of the 13th century, had a fundamental effect on conceptions of personal identity. With the breaking of the physically tangible link between producing and consuming, individuals, particularly those not involved in the economic process of work, and particularly those not allowed a significant political identity either, were freed to think of themselves as primarily centres of – at least, potential – consumption and enjoyment, an attitude which can be called 'bourgeois', in the strict sense. Women, therefore, particularly those from monied families and those living in religious communities, were the first to give literary expression to this new sense of the self. Mystical writers from Mechthild von Magdeburg (c. 1210–83) to the great Dominican theologian and spiritual director of women religious, Meister Eckhart (c. 1260–1327), found new linguistic and literary resources to describe the infinite, eternal, and unearned pleasure of the life of the soul with God: Eckhart coined some of the most important abstract words in the German language, including 'Bildung'. As literacy spread, the new concept of individual identity, reinforced by the practice of solitary and silent reading, rapidly made obsolete the chivalrous literature of feudalism, and after the rise of mysticism its themes survived only as the material of burlesque, of self-conscious revivalism, or of transformation into spiritual allegory. Outside the devotional realm much of the literature of the closely knit urban communities was collective or anonymous in origin: love songs, drinking songs, and ballads, later lumped together as 'folk songs', some of them still known today; liturgical and biblical dramas; the strictly regulated work of the literary guilds of artisans known as 'Mastersingers', most famous among them Hans Sachs (1494–1576). Narrative, whether in verse or prose, was often coarse, humorous, or obscene, and satirical in purpose. The collection of the exploits of the rogue Till Eulenspiegel ('Owleglasse') and the Low German animal epic

Reynard the Fox achieved European currency. New trends in the visual arts flowed in from the urban centres of Italy and the Low Countries and converged in the sculptor Tilman Riemenschneider (c. 1460–1531), and in Albrecht Dürer (1471–1528), the two artists of world stature produced by 15th-century Germany.

3. Tilman Riemenschneider, Apostles from the Altar of Our Lady in the Herrgottskirche, Creglingen, and faces of the 15th-century burghers who were Riemenschneider's patrons

The Ship of Fools (*Das Narrenschiff*, 1494) of Sebastian Brant (1457–1521), illustrated by Dürer, was the first German bestseller of the age of print. Johann Gutenberg's printing-press set up in Mainz around 1445 was the most influential contribution to world-culture made by the medieval German town, but in less than a century it was followed by another, almost equally important.

Both the main cultural tendencies of medieval German urban life, the mystical tendency and the realistic, came to a focus in Martin Luther (1483–1546), the son of a miner, who first trained as a lawyer and then became an Augustinian friar and professor of theology at the new university of Wittenberg.

Luther's teaching that God gave His heavenly rewards as a free gift in response to faith alone took to an extreme the mystics' dissociation of personal identity from the world of work. His Ninety-Five Theses (1517) against the papal practice of selling 'indulgences' – remission of the temporal punishment due to sin – were a passionate defence of the improbable belief (still prevalent today) that the soul is independent of the economic process. At the same time, like his near-contemporary Rabelais, Luther unashamedly spoke out for the material appetites that the towns had grown up to satisfy. His robust rejection of the poverty, chastity, and obedience to clerical authority to which he had originally vowed himself was expressed in the blunt, earthy, and satirical style of popular literature. He lived with equal intensity in the two worlds that monetarization had forced apart, and that the Catholic Church was struggling inadequately to hold together, and his revival of Augustine's distinction between the earthly and the heavenly cities was the true source of the modern dualism of matter and mind that is usually attributed to Descartes. His forceful yet divided personality marked all that he wrote, his pamphlets, sermons, catechisms, a handful of enormously influential hymns, and his translation of the Bible (1522–34),

AETHERNA IPSE SVAE MENTIS SIMVLACHRA LVTHERVS
EXPRIMIT·AT VVLTVS CERA LVCAE OCCIDVOS

·M·D·XX·

4. Luther as an Augustinian friar in 1520, by Lucas Cranach the Elder (1472–1553)

which made him into one of the founders of the modern German language.

But there had been reformers before Luther and if he had relied on the protection only of the towns whose culture he embodied Luther would have been burned at the stake like Jan Hus. Luther survived his condemnation by the Pope, and then by the Empire at the Reichstag held in Worms in 1521, because his cause was adopted by some of the German princes. For a prince of the Empire there were positive inducements to stand behind Luther as he faced down the authority of the Hapsburg Emperor Charles V: not just Luther's transfer of ultimate jurisdiction in religious matters from Rome to the local ruler (originally intended only as a temporary provision), nor even the consequential transfer of Church property to the state, but a more subtle and more significant advantage in the princes' continuing battle with the towns. For if the princes could cast themselves as the guardians of the modern urban and commercial sense of individual identity, expressed in the new Lutheran piety, the towns could be weaned away from their dependence on the Empire, which had originally given them their rights, and they would eventually find their home with their local overlords. Supporting these powerful forces was a dangerous game. Unlike Lutherans, Calvinists and Anabaptists believed in a right of resistance to sinful civil authority, and a bloody struggle between the various political and religious interests continued until the Peace of Augsburg in 1555. Luther had refused to compromise at Worms, but at Augsburg Lutheranism was more accommodating. The settlement was the basis of Germany's constitution for the next 250 years: the Empire was further weakened by the admission of a variety of confessions; the power of the princes was further enhanced by the right to determine the religion of their domains; and the freedom of the new Christian individuals was pared down to a right to emigrate to a territory of their own denomination.

The full historical drama of the Reformation, of its breach with the past in the interests of the individual soul and its satisfactions, was given symbolic, even mythical, form in an anonymous work of genius written for the new market created by the new technology of printing, the *History of Dr John Faust* (*Historia von D. Johann Fausten*) published in Frankfurt in 1587. There was a real Dr Faust, a rather unsuccessful astrologer and alchemist who came to an obscurely unnatural end around 1540, and the originality of the Frankfurt '*Volksbuch*' (chap-book), as it is usually called, lies primarily in its presenting itself as a piece of news – a 'novel' in the etymological sense – a story of and for its own time, not a retelling of a traditional tale nor even a traditional collection of comic episodes, though that is its superficial structure. Its hero, or villain, takes to a radical extreme the 16th century's rejection of tradition by abandoning established learning for magic and selling his soul to the enemy of religion in exchange for 24 years of pleasure, culminating in the resurrection of Helen of Troy to be his mistress. (By a quirk of literary fate, travelling English actors soon brought to Germany a dramatic version of the life of Dr Faust which Christopher Marlowe had prepared on the basis of the original chap-book, or its English translation, and which, in popularized and decreasingly recognizable adaptations for amateur productions or puppet plays, diffused the story through the whole of the non-literate German-speaking world.) A deep anxiety about the possible ultimate implications of the individualism on which Luther's revolt was based underlies both the transgressive thrill of the narration of Faust's excesses and the moralizing retreat at the end, after the devil has claimed his own, into the collective security of orthodox (Lutheran) church life. Just as Lutheranism compromised politically, accepting subordination to state authority in order to survive as a vehicle for personal salvation, so it compromised spiritually, imposing on itself a hierarchy and formulaic dogmatism as strict as Rome's, for fear of its own revolutionary, perhaps even self-destructive, potential. The towns in which the Reformation had been born had lost interest in innovation, whether in business or in religion. Instead, Lutheranism acquired a parallel history of mystics, eccentrics, and ultimately Pietists, who developed its original inspiration outside its established institutions. Many of them drew on the works of Jakob Böhme (1575–1624), a self-educated shoemaker from Görlitz, who sought to unify theology and natural philosophy by postulating triadic relations between positive and negative principles described in language as creative and neologistic as Meister Eckhart's, and partly derived from alchemy. Under the name of 'Behmen' he became known and influential in England, where his readers eventually included Newton and Blake.

After the great catastrophe of the Thirty Years War princely power was finally consolidated as the distinguishing feature of German political and cultural development in the modern era. The Peace of Westphalia of 1648 was little more than a secular extension of the Peace of Augsburg of a century before: the hour of absolutism and its culture had come. In Germany even Lutheran or Reformed monarchs had a clear interest in suppressing the independent spirit of Protestant towns. In the literary response to these profound changes an important role was played by Silesia (now southern Poland) where, after the Battle of the White Mountain in 1620, the victorious Hapsburgs, acting in their own domains as princes rather than emperors, reasserted central authority and pursued a vigorous policy of recatholicization. The predominantly Protestant German-speaking bourgeois of Silesia found themselves therefore on the fault-line between the opposing forces of the age, both in religion and in politics, between Catholic and Protestant, between the urban past and the absolutist future, and they first pointed out the path that German literature was to follow for the next three centuries. Martin Opitz (1597–1639), a man of few personal beliefs, toyed in public with the possibility of conversion to Catholicism, and, born the son of a master-butcher, became a distinguished diplomat in the service of various princes to whom he dedicated his books. He is usually regarded as the reformer who made modern German literature possible, on the strength of his *Book of German Poesy* (*Buch von der deutschen Poeterey*, 1624) which determined that German versification is based on stress, not the number or length of syllables, established the French alexandrine as the standard German metre, and laid down rules for rhymes and such forms as the ode and the sonnet. But his real achievement was to reconcile literature to the new political realities, 'for it is the greatest reward that poets can expect,' he wrote, 'that they find a place in the rooms of kings and princes' and his programme of regularization gave German verse a new prestige as a courtly art. His disciples included another Silesian, Andreas Gryphius (1616–64), author of tragedies and of some of the finest German sonnets. In both genres Gryphius embodied the Lutheran conflict of loyalties in a tension between powerful passions and the constraints of Opitzian form – as if the towns that had given Germany both material wealth and the Lutheran conscience were protesting at their slow and violent subjection to princely authority.

The greatest German writer of the 17th century, however, had no time for anyone's rules. Johann ('Hans') Jakob Christoffel von Grimmelshausen (1621 or 1622–76) came not from Silesia but from Gelnhausen near Frankfurt. When he was 12, his Protestant home town was sacked and burned and he became a soldier. After changing allegiance and religion, and finishing the war as secretary of an Imperial regiment, he eventually settled down as a land-agent for the Bishop of Strasbourg in a village in the Black Forest and adopted, with rather tenuous justification, a title of nobility. In his picaresque and partly autobiographical novel, *Adventures of the German Simplicissimus* (*Der abentheuerliche Simplicissimus Teutsch*, 1668 and 1671), we hear for the last time for many years the voice of a free and venturesome middle class, confident that it knows the facts of life as well as anyone, that though our ultimate destiny may not be in our own hands, it is not in anyone else's, and that it is up to us to make of it what we can. Scenes of war, grisly and comic, of urban, rural, and commercial life, of sexual intrigue in high and low places, of sheer supernatural fantasy, and one of Europe's first tales of shipwreck on a desert island, are combined, through the retrospective narration of the principal figure, now a hermit, into a complex moral fable of rise, fall, and redemption. *Simplicissimus* sold as no book of quality did in Germany for another hundred years and Grimmelshausen followed it up with a number of parallel stories from the same milieu. Notable among them are the memoirs of the female vagabond and camp-follower Courasche ('courage' – the name she gives to the pudenda by which she makes a living), whose childlessness only increases her sexual appetite and whose tales of warring and whoring, brutality and deceit, are uncompromised by any of Simplicissimus' moral and religious reflections. Her story stops, but does not end: Grimmelshausen was a realist and knew that a world without redemption does not admit of conclusions.

In the literature of the post-war period realism was in short supply. Outside the courts and the schools secular literature was a minority interest – in 1650 it made up only around 5% of all books published in Germany, while popular theology accounted for four times as many titles. Printed literature, volume produced for a market, the one form of cultural expression that is by its origins bourgeois and by its nature commercial, was firmly in the hands of state institutions, the church and the university. Though these figures changed hardly at all over the next 90 years, a movement in the atmosphere is detectable around 1680. In 1681, for the first time more books were published in German than in Latin, and in the 1670s, with the foundation of the first Pietist educational and charitable institutions in Frankfurt and Halle, Lutheranism began a revivalist mission to the world outside the ranks of the clergy and the universities. The original Lutheran focus on the inner life was rediscovered and a resource that had once been exclusive to mystics was redirected into more generally accessible channels. The middle classes were beginning to identify their souls as a place of freedom and were accepting their subordinate, but effective, role in a greater scheme of things. The new attitude was perfectly and profoundly expressed in the philosophy of Germany's outstanding intellectual genius of the time, Gottfried Wilhelm Leibniz (1646–1716), for whom the universe is a completely rational system, though its rationality is manifest only to those positioned on its higher levels, such as monarchs, and ultimately only to God. But every one of the units out of which the system is constructed is a soul completely secure in its own identity (a 'monad'), invulnerable to external events, and with a perspective on the whole which, though limited, is perfect in its own way and so a unique expression of the Divine wisdom. 'Know your place' is Leibniz' metaphysics and ethics in a nutshell, and they accorded well with the position of most German writers and thinkers in the age of absolutism.

(ii) Between France and England (1720–81)

Everyone knows that the 18th century was the century of Enlightenment. But there were (at least) two Enlightenments for by 1700 there were two distinct constituencies with an interest in criticizing what remained of Europe's feudal institutions. On the one hand, there was the bourgeois Enlightenment, characteristic of England and Scotland, but with some support in France, which criticized the established property owners, first the Church and then the nobility, in the interests of the free movement of capital, and in the name of the free individual. In philosophy the bourgeois Enlightenment – represented, for example, by Locke, Mandeville, and Newton – tended to empiricism, to giving the evidence of the senses priority over the speculations of reason, and ultimately to materialism. But, on the other hand, there was also what can be called an official, bureaucratic, or monarchical, Enlightenment which criticized the relics of feudalism, whether the Church and the nobility or the guilds and the Imperial Free Cities, in the name of collective order and in the interests of a single, central administrative will. The bureaucratic Enlightenment – represented, for example, by Descartes,

Leibniz, and Leibniz' influential disciple Christian August Wolff (1679–1754) – was usually associated with philosophical rationalism – with a tendency to give rational principles priority over the unreliable evidence of the individual's senses – and with the cultural authority of France, since France had become Europe's most powerful centralized monarchy. The rationalist Enlightenment of state officials was particularly strong in 18th-century Germany as local monarchs sought to tighten their grip, consolidating their territories and unifying their administration. A single transparent system was to rule in society as in thought, and the pupils of Wolff, whose system provided a rational argument from first principles for anything from the existence of God to the importance of coffee-shops, had a virtual monopoly on university appointments in philosophy throughout the middle years of the century. French, the international language of Enlightened monarchs, was the language of the German courts: the nobility conversed and corresponded in French, read French books, and at the court theatres often enough watched French plays. By contrast, until the mid-18th century, English had no international standing and the empiricist Enlightenment of the Anglo-Scottish bourgeoisie had few followers in German philosophy, its influence being felt more in the natural sciences and later in the study of history (particularly at the new university of Göttingen, founded in 1737 by the English King, George II, for the benefit of his German subjects in the Electorate of Hanover).

English literary influence was at its strongest in the northern ports of Hamburg and Bremen, which led an independent existence in semi-detachment from the rest of the Empire. The true bourgeois culture that maintained itself here produced the first German translation of *Robinson Crusoe*, in 1720, and the first German imitations of the supreme vehicles of middle-class enlightenment in England, the 'moral weeklies', such as Addison's *Spectator*. A cheerful sensualism, confident of the value of the material world, prevailed in the local literature, in the often humorous love poetry of the merchant Friedrich von Hagedorn (1708–54) or the voluminous meditations on flowers, insects, and other natural phenomena of the city-father Barthold Hinrich Brockes (1680–1747). But it was difficult to integrate this essentially exotic empiricism with the systematic rationalism that was emerging as the intellectual orthodoxy of princely Germany. An unwittingly, if disarmingly, comic element enters Brockes' verse when his conscientiously minute empirical observations ride up against the Wolffianism that assures him everything has a purpose in the Divine plan, and he concludes, for example, that the ultimate perfection of the chamois is that its horns can be made into handles for walking-sticks. The future of German literature had to lie in somewhere less marginal than Hamburg, somewhere where the challenge of the Enlightened absolutist state would be more directly felt and met – somewhere such as Leipzig. Leipzig was the largest city in Electoral Saxony and the home of a trade fair which, together with its counterpart in Frankfurt, had been a pillar of the German publishing industry since the 16th century, but it was neither a Free City nor a centre of government. (The Elector and his court resided at Dresden, 70 miles away.) The majority of its citizens were as bourgeois as Hamburg's but they did not manage their own affairs. Leipzig, however, differed from the Imperial Free Cities in a further crucial respect: it had a university. Some of the most active members of Germany's subject middle class here lived alongside the most distinctive cultural institution of Protestant absolutism. In the second quarter of the 18th century, Leipzig was the centre of a powerful campaign to make literature in German the preferred means of cultural self-expression for a middle class, whether commercial or official, united in its acceptance of subordination to princely authority. The campaign was consciously modelled on that of Opitz, but it was in the hands, not of a diplomat and intimate of rulers, seeking a hearing for poetry in the chambers of the great, but of a professor of poetry (unpaid) and logic (paid). Johann Christoph Gottsched (1700–66) was the author of a two-volume compendium of the Leibniz-Wolffian philosophy and, in the spirit of that philosophy, he tried to show, in his *Essay towards a Critical Art of Poetry*

*for the Germans (Versuch einer Critischen Dichtkunst vor die
Deutschen*, 1730), how literature could and should be based
on a few simple, rational principles, systematically applied, so
that the same works could be enjoyed by the bourgeoisie and by
university-educated civil servants. He concentrated therefore,
not on the novel, the new genre developed during his lifetime by
Defoe, Fielding, and Richardson for mass circulation among the
English middle classes, and translated for the German market
in suspiciously Anglophile Hamburg and Göttingen, but on the
drama. Unlike the novel, the drama had a good classical and
academic pedigree, and a central role in the culture of the courts,
yet it still provided a measure of general entertainment. Gottsched
opened up the drama as a channel of cultural communication
between rulers and ruled in absolutist Germany. He insisted on
the use of the German language, established personal links with
such touring theatre companies as survived, and in collaboration
with his wife wrote, collected, and translated model plays for
them. But he also demanded that plays be rationally constructed
and observe the unities and proprieties of the French drama of
the age of Louis XIV, so making a play in German a conceivable
alternative, in a court theatre, to a tragedy by Racine or an opera
in Italian. Gottsched created a powerful idea, which continued to
dominate the discussion long after his own applications of it had
become ridiculous. But the novel, or rather, the developing book
market which fed the demand for the novel, could not be ignored,
and Gottsched did more by publishing plays, and collections
of plays, as books to be read than by all his prescriptions for
theatrical writing and performance.

German literature of the 18th century emerged not from the
imitation of works of the English empiricist Enlightenment
nor from Gottsched's Leibniz-Wolffian and France-oriented
rationalism but from the conflict of the two, a conflict which
mirrored the diverging interests of the official and the bourgeois
wings of the German middle class, and which intensified as
the century wore on. The direct opposition to Gottsched was

concentrated in two areas of self-governing republicanism, Bremen in the north and Switzerland in the south, where the poetry of the anti-monarchist Milton, rich in depictions of the supernatural, was hailed as the counter-example to rationalism. The creative compromise between Gottsched and Milton was found, however, by a brilliant theology student in Leipzig, Friedrich Gottlieb Klopstock (1724–1803). In 1748 Klopstock published the first three cantos of *The Messiah* (*Der Messias*), a would-be Miltonic epic on the theme that had defeated Milton, the redemptive action of Christ, and written in hexameters, the metre of Homer and Virgil, previously little used in German. Klopstock went on to adapt Greek and Latin strophic forms in his 'odes', and these shorter poems on love, friendship, nature, and moral and patriotic themes – and the pleasures of ice-skating, for which he had a passion – show, better than his epic, the truly revolutionary feature of his writing: a new conception of the seriousness and autonomy of literature. He was committed to the commercial medium of the printed and published word, not to Gottsched's semi-courtly medium of the theatre, but he was claiming for what he wrote an authority equal to that of the state institutions of the university (which provided the scholarly basis for his formal innovations) and of the Church (which gave him the subject matter of *The Messiah* and the theological language of his other poems). In Klopstock's odes, however, the purpose of the frequent invocations of God and immortality is not to explore a religious mystery, but to underline the unique significance that attaches to his experience and his feelings simply because they are his, and because – as the strange and monumental form tells us – he is a poet. The anxious, slightly puzzled, naturalist who recounted his quest for order in Brockes' poems was replaced by a consciousness that knew itself to be the source of the meaning it found in a landscape, a thunderstorm, a summer's night. The shape of things to come became apparent when, on the publication of the first cantos of *The Messiah*, a patron emerged who was willing to underwrite this claim to exceptionality. The king of Denmark granted

Klopstock a pension so that the epic could be completed and he gave up his theological studies to become Germany's first full-time poet.

If poetry became the religion of Klopstock, Greek art became the religion of another ex-theologian, Johann Joachim Winckelmann (1717–68), who escaped altogether from the Germany that offered him only the drudgery of schoolmastering and tutoring to devote himself to the study of ancient art in Rome. In *Thoughts on the Imitation of the Greek Works of Painting and Sculpture* (*Gedanken über die Nachahmung der griechischen Werke in der Malerei und Bildhauerkunst*, 1755), he argued that the physical and moral beauty that we find in the art of the ancient Greeks derives from the merits of their society and religion; by imitating their art we can hope to recover those ancient perfections. The 'noble simplicity and calm grandeur', as his famous phrase has it, of their best works can suffuse our art, and lives, and – the implication seems to follow – our society and religion too. His ecstatic descriptions of particular works, above all the Belvederean Apollo, use the language of Pietist enthusiasm to suggest that through his own feelings and words the spirit of the ancient deities has re-awoken to become active in the modern world. As yet poetry and the visual arts were not understood as branches of the same human activity – what we now call 'Art' – but once they had both begun to be seen as alternative secular channels of divine revelation a first step had been taken towards a general aesthetic theory. (The term 'aesthetics' itself entered academic currency in 1750 as an invention of the Prussian disciple of Wolff, Alexander Gottlieb Baumgarten [1714–62].)

Among the German middle classes, however, the most widely disseminated substitute for the institutional religion that was so closely associated with princely dominance was in the mid-18th century neither poetry nor the visual arts, but an intense interest in personal feelings. The inner sanctum of pre-social identity,

5. Wieland, the model 18th-century man of letters, at his writing desk, 1806

which Pietism called the soul, and Leibnizianism called the monad, was given a secular form as the power of having emotions, and here at least the individual could feel master of his or her fate. Men and women alike found themselves in Laurence Sterne's *A Sentimental Journey* (1768), so that its German translation almost immediately provided the name of their culture of tears: '*Empfindsamkeit*', 'Sentimentalism'.

Their mentor was Christoph Martin Wieland (1733–1813), though not all of Wieland's readers perceived the extent to which his refined materialism undermined the security of their inner fastness. Another son of a pastor who was early troubled by religious doubts, after translating Shakespeare he eventually found his literary metier: the novel, or romance, set in an imaginary world, usually a schematic and sunlit classical antiquity, in which an amusing plot, psychologically subtle and flirtatiously erotic, was recounted by a shrewd and ironical narrator. It was a compromise with the manner of Fielding, perfectly attuned to German circumstances. No risks were run through any direct representation of contemporary reality, but a kind of realism was none the less achieved. The effects of human emotions on the mind, on moral, philosophical, and political attitudes, were analysed with great delicacy in these novels (notably *Agathon*, first edition 1767), in Wieland's exquisite verse narratives (for example, *Musarion*, 1768), and in his letters. He was at the centre of a Germany-wide web of letter-writers who exchanged with each other thoughts and feelings, and thoughts about feelings, occasioned by the incidents of their uneventful lives or by the books they were reading (whether religious or, with increasing likelihood, not). The balance that, with a deceptive appearance of ease, he achieved between sense and reason in his thinking, and in his writing between imported and native traditions, Wieland also achieved in his personal affairs between officialdom and private enterprise. In 1769 he was appointed to a professorship of philosophy at the little university of Erfurt and three years later he accepted the invitation of Anna Amalia, regent of the nearby duchy of Saxe-Weimar, to become tutor to her son Karl August, who was approaching his majority. Wieland took the Duchess's shilling and settled in Weimar but he did not lose his independence. In 1773 he began a literary newspaper *Der Teutsche Merkur* (*The German Mercury*), in which his correspondence network went over seamlessly into print. It became the most successful periodical in southern Germany, and, though he eventually retired from full-time editorship, it provided him with a supplementary income for the rest of his long and productive life.

The Seven Years War, which in 1763 appeared to conclude with the triumph of the Protestant interest, inaugurated in Germany a new and more turbulent phase of cultural transformation. The greatly heightened prestige of English culture after the war meant easier access to a free-thinking and individualist Enlightenment, which increased the friction between intellectuals and the social and political structure of absolutist Germany. Gotthold Ephraim Lessing (1729–81), for example, was the son of a pastor and studied theology in Leipzig, but the combined influences of English deism and of Gottsched's favourite troupe of actors led him to abandon a clerical career for the uncertain life of a literary freelance. Having written plays since his teens he had his first major success in 1755 with *Miss Sara Sampson*, virtually a manifesto for the English style. This first German, or 'bourgeois' tragedy (*bürgerliches Trauerspiel*), with its indecisive seducer, virtuous victim, and sorrowing father, was an implausible attempt to put on the stage the Richardsonian multi-volume novel of sentiment. To that extent it subscribed to Gottsched's view that the drama, not the novel, was to be the means of literary self-expression for the German middle classes. But in 1759 Lessing carried out the most effective literary assassination in the German language when in a single issue of his periodical he dismissed Gottsched's 'reforms', put Shakespeare in the place of Gottsched's French models, and pointed German writers looking for authentic local material to the home-grown story of Dr Faust (whom he envisaged as an Enlightenment seeker after truth, who could certainly not be condemned to eternal punishment). In the immediate aftermath of the war Lessing then wrote a comedy which confirmed both his commitment to a realist literature of contemporary life and his distaste for the politics of Frederick the Great, whose campaigns had brought Silesia to Prussia but had devastated Dresden, Leipzig, and the Saxon economy: *Minna von Barnhelm* (published 1767) is the earliest German play to have been continuously in the repertoire since its publication, though its sardonic undertones have not always been appreciated. Lessing seemed in the 1760s to be German literature's most radical voice, indeed he was helping to redefine what literature was. As an ex-theologian, struggling to find himself a niche in the private sector, and opposed to the authoritarianism of either state or church, he represented all the social interests that might lie behind a shift from rationalism to empiricism, and from French to English models. But he knew the precariousness of his position. In 1766 he published a theoretical treatise, *Laocöon*, which purported to differentiate literature from painting, but thereby implied an initial comparability between them and so prepared the way for the view that they were both after all only variations on the same human activity that would soon be known as 'Art'. The ambiguity – was literature a power in its own right or did it belong with such other adornments of court life as the visual arts? – reflected Lessing's awareness of his vulnerable social position and of the possibility that in Germany literature might not be able to establish itself as an economically and politically independent cultural authority. He spent the next three years as the house playwright for a doomed attempt by the Hamburg bourgeoisie to set up their own 'National Theatre'. After its collapse he accepted that only if he compromised his principles could he make the decent living that would allow him to marry and settle down, and in 1770 he entered princely service as the librarian of the Duke of Brunswick in Wolfenbüttel. His last tragedy, *Emilia Galotti* (1772), was a bitter farewell to his earlier life, a story of the corrupting effect of absolute power both on the prince who wields it and on his middle-class victims, whose only defence against him is moral and physical self-destruction.

The achievement of literary greatness through a disappointed love-affair with England was the unexpected outcome of the career of Georg Christoph Lichtenberg (1742–99), Germany's most prominent natural scientist (he was professor of physics in Göttingen and the teacher of Gauss), and an entertaining and effective satirist of various fashionable intellectual follies. A subject of George III, whom he knew personally, he twice visited what he called 'the Isles of the Blessed', and admired English science, industry, literature, and political institutions. All his life he gathered materials for a comic novel in the English manner but what his literary executors found was far better than any completed pastiche of Fielding or Sterne would have been: the commonplace books in which day by day he had recorded ideas, fragments, reflections, turns of phrase, the first, most varied, and most personal German collection of aphorisms, a form in which the English have never excelled:

> In many a work of a famous man I would rather read what he cut out than what he has left in.

> When he saw a midge fly into the candle and it now lay in the throes of death he said: 'Down with the bitter cup, you poor creature, a professor is watching, and is sorry for you.'

> English geniuses go on ahead of fashion and German geniuses come along behind it.

If only Germany too could have a free and active middle class, outward-looking and confidently realistic, individualistic to the point, if necessary, of eccentricity, and with a literature, and especially with novels, to match! That longing was the energy that powered the literary turmoil of the 1760s and 1770s, which has become known by the title of one of the minor plays it produced, *Sturm und Drang* (Storm and Stress). The theorist of the movement, Johann Gottfried Herder (1744–1803), an East Prussian from what is now Poland, spent his life in struggle with the dominant forces of secularization and absolutism. Despite a serious crisis of faith in the early 1770s he refused to bow to the authority of deist critique and remained a clergyman, but though therefore a state official he maintained a middle-class hostility to monarchs. He envisaged, but never quite achieved, a synthesis of aesthetics, theology, and the rapidly expanding field of cultural anthropology, which he was one of the first to attempt to organize: indeed, his conviction that the material circumstances of a people's life, their skills, language, beliefs and artistic and literary practices, make up a single self-sufficient and characteristic whole was instrumental in forming the modern concept of a 'culture'. It was Leibnizian monadism applied to history. Individual human beings too, he thought, have a unique character, an 'original genius', which particularly through the medium of language can become a people's common possession. Literature, whether sacred or secular, is a tissue of individual and collective genius. Shakespeare was a 'dramatic God', a maker of worlds, but he could not be detached from the English culture which had formed him and which he then helped to form. It followed that Germany could not acquire a national literature like that of England or France merely by imitating English or French models: Germany had to identify and draw on its own resources, on its medieval past, its popular entertainments, its folk song. At Strasbourg university in the winter of 1770–1 Herder met the man he thought capable of that task: Johann Wolfgang Goethe (1749–1832).

Goethe was exceptional among 18th-century German writers, and not just in his abilities: at least as a young man, he had no need to write for money, or even to work at all. He was a true bourgeois, a member of the upper middle class of the Imperial Free City of Frankfurt. His mother was the daughter of the town clerk, his father lived on his capital, and he studied law – first at Leipzig (where he met Gottsched) and then at Strasbourg – more in order to occupy than to advance himself. He was spared the anxieties and necessities which drove his contemporaries into a creative compromise with their political masters and he might eventually have been lost to literature altogether. But Herder showed him how the traditions of the late-medieval and early-modern German towns that he embodied met the literary need of the moment and could in him re-enter the mainstream. On his return to Frankfurt, having proclaimed to his friends his conversion to Shakespeare, Goethe completed in six weeks the first draft of a prose chronicle play, unlike anything in German before it, with 59 changes of scene, based on the memoirs of the early 16th-century robber baron Götz von Berlichingen, and with a cameo part for Martin Luther. He became increasingly interested in the 16th century, when German urban culture had been of European significance, he studied Hans Sachs and imitated his verse, and like Lessing he began to think of re-dramatizing the story of Dr Faust. Goethe's Strasbourg experience was, fundamentally, and thanks to Herder, linguistic: the discovery of the literary potential of the language of ordinary people outside the established educational, cultural, and political institutions. There is nothing like the language of the best scenes in *Götz von Berlichingen* (published 1773) in French or English literature of the time, except perhaps in the work of Robert Burns. A few acquaintances shared his experience and inspiration, notably Jakob Michael Reinhold Lenz (1751–92) and Heinrich Leopold Wagner (1747–79), and they were the creative core of the Storm and Stress movement, though others made more noise.

Goethe's greatness lay, however, in his ability to bring together all the strands of contemporary intellectual life (and in his being free to do so). In the 1770s and early 1780s, he poured out a cornucopia of lyrical poems, many of them the inspiration of a moment, some left unpublished for years, and nearly all of them unique in form: ballads, imitations of folk song, rhymed fragments that catch an emotion on the wing, full-length odes, mysterious chants, and unclassifiable poetic responses to – rather than meditations on – life, God, love, and Nature, some only half-emerged from the context of a letter or a diary. They have become some of his best-known works, not least because of their appeal to generations of composers. They are the product not just of the new intimacy with the spoken German language and German popular traditions that he gained in Strasbourg and of his intuitive response to Shakespeare's symbolic use of natural imagery, but also of a confidence, learned from Klopstock, in the vivifying poetic consciousness, and of an openness to the Pietist and Sentimentalist practice of self-scrutiny. Goethe sought and cultivated friendships through the Sentimentalist network, of which his own correspondence quickly became a valued part. An instinct seems to have told him that Wieland's path of compromise had more future in Germany than any attempt to set up an autonomous middle-class culture, and he became increasingly aware of the tragic potential in the movement which saw him as the growing-point, or even the 'Messiah', of German literature. *Götz von Berlichingen* is an ambiguous play, and not just because its hero's iron hand is a symbol both of strength and of emasculation. It tells two stories, one of Götz, who spends his life fighting to arrest the course of history and defend the old freedoms of the Holy Roman Empire, and one of his *alter ego*, Weislingen, who throws in his lot with the rising power of princely absolutism. But the zestful energy of the story-telling, by a poet in love with his subject matter, conceals that both life-plans end in a cul-de-sac: Götz fades away into admonitory irrelevance; Weislingen succumbs to his own inner divisions. *Götz* was one of the first consciously 'historical' works of imaginative literature and it was an important model for Walter Scott, who translated it. But its themes of political conflict and personal destiny belonged to Goethe's own time and generation, and in his next major work he succeeded in incorporating those themes into a realistic depiction of contemporary life, not in the compromise form of a virtually unstageable drama, but in the modern form *par excellence*, in a novel.

The Sorrows of Young Werther (*Die Leiden des jungen Werther*, 1774) made Goethe a European name, though the novel's tragic plot depends on specifically German circumstances (and was based on a real event). It is a novel in letters, but since the letters all come from Werther and say nothing about their addressees they appear to be written to the book's readers, who are thereby invited to see themselves as a circle of correspondents and Werther as one of their own. Even now the novel has an extraordinary power to draw its readers into the intoxicating logic of Werther's hyperactive sensibility: the swings of mood in his response to the natural world; his obsessive love for Lotte, engaged, and then married, to another man; the disintegration of his mind as an 'Editor' steps in to piece together the evidence for the last days and hours before he shoots himself. What might make the book seem dated is actually the reason for its continuing modernity: for all the importance in it of the idea of 'Nature', it represents feelings not simply as spontaneous but as furnished to its characters, and to its readers too, by culture – by books and fashions. Its realism is social, even in matters of the mind. Werther wears the clothes and boots of an English country gentleman to demonstrate both his personal integrity and his independence of court and university and he and Lotte know they are soulmates because they both react to a thunderstorm with a reminiscence of the same ode by Klopstock. Werther's story is therefore not simply the story of the self-destruction of a pathological individual, but like Emilia Galotti – and Lessing's play is open beside him when he dies – he is driven to his death by social and political constraints as well. Halfway through his 'affair' with Lotte he attempts to escape from his emotions by taking a job as a state official. However, he has enough money – he is enough of a true bourgeois – not to be kept in the job by financial necessity and he soon feels driven out of it, and back to his obsession with Lotte, by the exclusivism of the ruling nobility, who see in him a representative of the new class of upstart intellectual. With a specificity the brilliance of which has faded little with time, *Werther* recounts the failure, in hostile economic

51

and political conditions, of the bid from that class to establish a culture of its own on an English model. But the novel also shows the consequences of failure: the danger that the Sentimentalism which was the only alternative to revolt would run out of control and feeling would become detached from any external reality, even from life.

Werther destroys only himself. But the revolt of the 'geniuses', as those around Goethe were soon called, could extract a price from others too. At the same time as he was writing *Werther* Goethe was thinking about the 16th century again. But the version of the Faust legend that he was drafting was far from being a historical drama like *Götz*. He envisaged a 'new' *Faust* in which a light historical varnish would ease the introduction of a few unavoidable supernatural elements into an essentially modern plot. Apart from its first three scenes, which show Faust as a magician who, in some unexplained way, acquires a diabolical companion, Mephistopheles, Goethe's first draft of his life's work – usually called *Urfaust* ('the original *Faust*') – is an 18th-century seduction narrative which owes much to Richardson and little to the original chap-books and plays. There is no warrant in the tradition for the story of Faust's liaison with a town-girl, Margarete ('Gretchen' is an affectionate diminutive), unless she is seen as this modern Faust's modern Helen, as Goethe at one time probably intended. Goethe's play is quite different, however, from other seduction stories of the time – *Miss Sara Sampson*, for example. The difference lies, firstly, in the character and motivation of the seducer. The first scenes are not detachable from the rest of the action: Faust is no philanderer, his love-affair with Gretchen is a fulfilment of the passionate urge he expresses in his opening monologue to leave behind the cerebral world of mere thought and embrace with all his senses the full human lot. He turns his back on the university – the only trace of princely Germany in the play's social setting – and seeks reality in the life of the town, first in its taverns and then in the little world of its hard-working but contented, Catholic, inhabitants who seem untroubled by the yearnings that torment him, a free thinker, and probably a (former) Protestant. Yet his disquiet echoes their deeper needs too: because Gretchen can recognize in Faust the promise of some unknown, but not unreal, fulfilment she can respond to him in desire, while Faust's desire for her, at first simply sensual, turns to love. The sympathetic realism with which her relatively lowly milieu is depicted – her sparsely furnished room, her homely turns of phrase, the gossip of her neighbours – has few parallels in contemporary literature (Goldsmith perhaps); the stark tragedy of her desperation in pregnancy, her alienation from her family, her infanticide, madness, and condemnation to a death she still fears, has none. The malignant presence of Mephistopheles, who rejoices in her undoing, extends her tragedy to Faust. Her end seems to be her lover's too and the revolt of this modern Faust seems, like that of his original, to lead him down to Hell, cast out even by the world with which he has fallen in love. But the significance of this simple story, simply told, is enlarged and transfigured as Goethe pours into it all the resources of the poems he was writing at the time. Each of the concise, individual, almost disconnected scenes has its own mood, and most have their own time of day. The feeling soul, whose insistent longing for reality is imperiously articulated by Faust, enters into the texture of the play. The powerful visual themes around which the scenes are built up – Faust's magic book, Gretchen combing her hair or offering flowers to the Madonna – are enhanced by the rich imagery and rhythmic variety of Faust's visions and Gretchen's haunting songs, and by the terrible plausibility of her final ramblings in prose. A bitter story of cultural defeat is transformed by Goethe's poetry into a true tragedy of love and betrayal, ambition and guilt.

Lenz and Wagner, who both also treated the theme of the infanticide mother, shared Goethe's empathy for popular speech, though without his ability to turn it into poetry. Lenz, however, achieved something almost as remarkable: his plays *The Tutor* (*Der Hofmeister*, 1774) and *The Soldiers* (*Die Soldaten*, 1776) are virtually novels about contemporary Germany. Dramatic structure is dissolved into a kaleidoscope of plots and snapshot scenes, but the dramatic form is used to create an extraordinary objectivity. Lenz ruthlessly strips out any compromise with Sentimentalism and the monadic tradition: his characters have no inner life but are shown as functioning social mechanisms, manipulating each other through language. They may appear to be grotesques but they are still capable of suffering, and Lenz was as aware as Goethe of the tragic potential in his society. Läuffer, the tutor, in his play of that name, is an exemplar of the class of unemployed ex-theologians (Lenz himself was one) out of which German literature, and the Storm and Stress, emerged. But Läuffer is no Faust. He falls in love with his charge and caught between inescapable desire and equally inescapable oppression he gives up the struggle and emasculates himself. The failed revolt, a theme of many works of the Storm and Stress, was a historical reality though no one represented its true character as directly and painfully as Lenz. Lenz himself succumbed to mental illness, and most of his fellow-writers emigrated or otherwise fell silent.

Goethe, however, did not give up, though he considered emigration to Switzerland. In 1775 he did transplant himself, but within Germany. He broke off his work on *Egmont*, a play he had started to write on the 16th-century Dutch revolt against Spanish absolute rule, followed Wieland's example, and settled in Weimar at the invitation of Duke Karl August, now 18 years old. At his suggestion Herder was summoned shortly afterwards to become the spiritual head of the duchy's Lutheran Church. Goethe's move from bourgeois Frankfurt was an acceptance of reality, of the primacy of princely Germany, and it both coincided with the peak of Storm and Stress and marked its passing. 1776 anyway put an end to the mid-century outburst of Anglophilia. Once England was at war with its American colonies it could no longer be represented simply as the land of the free. There was no longer an obvious external model for those who felt oppressed by conditions at home, and no longer an easy choice between the culture of the towns and the culture of the princes or between the empiricist and the rationalist Enlightenment. Germany would have to find its own way out of its internal conflicts. In 1776 two high-voltage plays – *The Twins* (*Die Zwillinge*) by Friedrich Maximilian Klinger (1752–1831) and the more nuanced *Julius von Tarent* by Johann Anton Leisewitz (1752–1806) – gave expression to this new, or newly acute, dilemma, by means of the same dramatic motif: the murderous strife of two brothers. At the same time a rebellious schoolboy in Stuttgart, Friedrich Schiller (1759–1805), began drafting the definitive treatment of the theme, his first play, *The Robbers* (*Die Räuber*), which took the reading public by storm on its publication in 1781, and reduced its audience to sobs and swoons when it was first performed the following year.

Like the two wings of the German middle class, the bourgeois and the officials, Schiller's two brothers are united by what divides them: they are both potential successors to the *ancien régime* represented by their father, the almost permanently moribund Count von Moor. Karl, the legitimate heir, has a high ethical sense but while at university is tricked into revolt by his younger brother, Franz. Franz, a materialist, determinist, and would-be atheist, puts on an appearance of subservience but is plotting not only to supplant his brother but to kill their father. Karl's crimes as leader of a robber band, however, prove more real and more numerous than those of Franz and when the Count finally dies both brothers are equally responsible. But the succession falls to neither, for both have committed suicide – Franz literally, and Karl in effect, by surrendering himself to the power of the law, in order to expiate his wrongdoing. The moral authority of the dead father is the sole survivor of two collapsed insurrections, though it is unclear in what form that authority can now be embodied, since all existing legal institutions have been denounced as hopelessly corrupt. A modern, international audience can still be gripped by the story of Karl and his band, a prescient analysis of the logic of self-righteous terrorism in a moral void. The huge success of the play in Germany in its own time and subsequently was no

Iffland als Franz Moor.
Act. V. S. I.

6. August Wilhelm Iffland (1759–1814), playwright and actor-director, as Franz Moor in the first performance of Schiller's *The Robbers*

doubt due to the ferocity with which it dramatized the conflict between the two value-systems available to the middle class in its struggle against princely rule – self-interested materialism or university-educated idealism – while it left prudently unassailed the structure of power itself. The future seemed to lie with a suitably chastened Karl rather than the rapaciously individualist Franz. Schiller's late version of Storm and Stress was free of any hankerings after England and largely unaffected by Herder's and Goethe's desire to revive older German culture, especially that of the towns. Instead Schiller focussed, with the penetrating clarity of a born dramatist, on the political and moral fault-lines in his contemporary society. With *The Robbers* an independent modern German literary tradition begins.

Chapter 3
The age of idealism (1781–1832)

(i) A republic of letters (1781–1806)

1781 was a remarkable year. It saw the publication not only of *The Robbers* but of another work destined to have an even deeper and wider effect on German culture, *Critique of Pure Reason* (*Kritik der reinen Vernunft*) by Immanuel Kant (1724–1804). 'No man of learning', Goethe later wrote, 'has with impunity rejected, opposed, or disdained the great philosophical movement begun by Kant'. Kant had been through his own version of the crisis that in literature culminated in Storm and Stress, but unlike the poets he had spent the 1770s publishing nothing, just thinking and writing. He was free to do so because in 1770, after 15 years as a private teacher of Wolffianism, he had at last been appointed to a salaried professorial chair in the university of Königsberg. But at about the same time he was confronted with the challenge of the radically sceptical empiricism of David Hume, which seemed to put into question his life's work so far. In the ten years of thought that followed Kant endeavoured to reconcile the empiricist Enlightenment of the bourgeoisie with the rationalist Enlightenment of the officials in a new fusion to which he gave the name of Idealism. Kant believed he had shown that something like the Leibniz-Wolffian rational order of things is implied or presupposed by what we can know of the world through our senses: we cannot know that order directly, because it is the precondition of our knowing anything at all, but it furnishes the ideal, or pattern, to which we have to approximate what we do know. Knowledge has to have both an empirical content and a rational form. Kant achieves this result by a re-examination of the relation in our experience between the subjective and the objective (terms that acquired their modern sense in German academic philosophy in his lifetime), which he compares to the Copernican revolution in astronomy. Just as Copernicus argued that we saw movement in the sky not because the stars move but because the earth moves, so, Kant implies, he has shown, without changing the appearance of the natural or moral world, that some of its basic features are to be attributed to the observer, not to the observed, to the subject, not to the object. We cannot know things as they are in themselves, we can know them only as they appear to us, mediated through our perceptual and mental apparatus, and acquiring on the way an aspiration to a necessary and rational structure. In his theory of knowledge Kant carefully balances the claims of the sensuous and the particular against the claims of the rational and universal. In his moral theory, similarly, he balances the – apparently radically individualist – assertion that only the free actions of a self-determining agent, unaffected by external influences, can count as moral against the equally emphatic assertion that freedom is not freedom to do what you like but freedom to impose on yourself a universal law. This subtle compromise between two different Enlightenments provided an ideological basis on which the German official class could claim to represent and harmonize the interests both of the economically productive middle class and of the absolute monarch, or state, which they served. By the mid-1790s, Kantians had completely displaced Wolffians in the chairs of philosophy in German universities. The period of officialdom's cultural hegemony – the age of philosophical idealism – was the period in which German literature bore its most distinctive fruits, its classical age.

The year 1781 was also marked by another milestone: the death of Lessing. His life after he settled in Wolfenbüttel foreshadowed what was to come. His publication of an exhaustive critique of the New Testament left in manuscript by the previous librarian led to a virulent controversy with the Lutheran hierarchy, which expanded from theological issues to include the freedom of the press and was abruptly terminated by the fiat of the Duke of Brunswick, his sovereign and employer. Lessing's response was to shift the conflict on to less exposed terrain. He returned to the drama to create an altogether new kind of play in *Nathan the Wise* (*Nathan der Weise*, 1779), which he called a 'dramatic poem' because it was written in blank verse and was to be published as a book, since he did not expect it to be produced in a theatre. Set in Jerusalem at the time of the Crusades, *Nathan* is a comedy which purports to show the achievement of mutual tolerance between representatives of Judaism, Christianity, and Islam. In fact they recognize rather that they all share a fourth, rational, religion, which refrains from judging the truth of any of the acknowledged faiths and constitutes a kind of secret freemasonry of those 'for whom it is enough to be called human'. *Nathan the Wise* is the prototype of the German 'classical' drama of the next hundred years: a play in verse, written to be read as much as to be performed, on a philosophical or moral theme that reinterprets or secularizes a theological issue, and with an elite rather than a popular appeal – *Nathan* is, among other things, about elitism and represents, in its principal characters, the audience for the genre that it founds.

Lessing's development from freelance to ducal employee is reflected in Schiller's career after the success of *The Robbers*. Faced with a complete prohibition on any further writing from the autocratic Duke of Württemberg, who had already forced him away from theology into service as a regimental surgeon, Schiller fled his homeland for Mannheim where he became resident playwright at the theatre which had first produced him. He wrote two more plays on the problems of revolt and political succession, one of which, *Intrigue and Love* (*Kabale und Liebe*, 1784), made effective theatre out of the contemporary German material in which Lenz had specialized. In a telling sub-plot, a tragic farewell to obsolete Anglophilia, the hero discovers in the English mistress of his prince not the corrupt handmaid of tyranny he had imagined (the prince has sold his subjects as mercenaries to fight in the American war) but a spirit of the liberty which he is fated not to enjoy. Even though his contract in Mannheim was not renewed Schiller resolved to continue the attempt to earn his living from literature, editing journals and writing historical works while he struggled to give shape to his next play, *Don Carlos* (1787), a grand and over-complex historical drama in verse. Only the generosity of friends in Leipzig and Dresden rescued him from penury. He put out feelers to Weimar, where his fiancée had been brought up, and in 1789, partly thanks to Goethe, he was given an unsalaried professorship of history at the nearby university of Jena and a small pension from Duke Karl August which enabled him to marry. A much more generous grant from the Crown Prince of Denmark allowed him to devote himself to the study of Kant at a point when overwork had undermined his health, and for a while he transformed himself into a philosopher. Schiller was disappointed that Kant did not have a theory of beauty which gave a proper dignity and importance to the literature to which he was, in every sense, devoting his life. (Kant had a good reason for not having such a theory: he thought nothing could, by definition, be more important than morality, doing what was right, and what he said about beauty was deliberately designed to prevent the slide from aesthetic into moral and theological language that had been encouraged by talk of poets as 'creators' and genius as 'god-like'). Picking up a metaphor that was common in the circle around Goethe Schiller started to treat literature as a kind of 'art', and in a number of studies – notably *On the Aesthetic Education of Humanity in a Series of Letters* (*Über die ästhetische Erziehung des Menschen in einer Reihe von Briefen*, 1795) – he developed a systematic account of beauty as the sensuous manifestation of moral freedom, and so of artists as the moral liberators and educators of the human race. Armed with this flattering theory he approached Goethe, who had hitherto kept him at a distance, with the proposal that they should jointly edit a new literary journal, *The Horae* (*Die Horen*, 1795-7).

Goethe had originally seen in the author of *The Robbers*, with its vision of Germany as a place of hopeless and unproductive conflict, the representative of everything he was trying to escape when he came to Weimar in 1775. But their different developments led them on convergent paths. Goethe had begun life in Weimar by cutting himself off completely from the commercial book-trade (in which he had earned a lot of money for the pirate publishers, but none for himself). For ten years, he published almost nothing, giving himself instead to the small world of administration and court life (he was made a Privy Councillor, and ennobled) and to a semi-tutorial relationship with his friend and patron, the young duke. He continued to write but completed little beyond the first version of a play, *Iphigenia in Tauris* (1779 and 1786-7), in prose, but in the courtly French form approved by Gottsched, on the healing power of a resolute faith in the goodness of things. That faith was severely tried as the duchy came to seem constricted and unreformable and as his poetry all but dried up, but in 1786 in desperation he broke out: he fulfilled a lifelong ambition to follow Winckelmann and travel to Rome, and he returned to publishing by signing a contract to bring out a collected edition of his writings. Over the next few years he completely changed the basis of his presence in Weimar, withdrawing from his originally total commitment to a princely court and rebalancing his relationship with the middle-class reading public. His visit to Rome turned into a two-year sabbatical, spent enjoying the art and landscape of Italy and the life of the German artists' colony, from which he returned with reluctance; he persuaded the Duke to relieve him of his administrative duties and treat him first and foremost 'as a poet'; he completed his edition, finishing *Egmont* and *Torquato Tasso*, the first tragedy with a poet as its hero, and putting *Iphigenia* into fluent blank verse; and to the horror of titled Weimar he set up house with a middle-class woman, Christiane Vulpius (1765–1816), who bore him several children of whom only a son survived infancy. Karl August, however, expected something in exchange for the salary on which Goethe, despite his private means, had come to rely, and from 1791 put his poet in charge of his theatre. Goethe did his duty, but with mixed feelings. Drama had been his medium in the time of Storm and Stress, which he had now put behind him, and theatre as court entertainment had little appeal when he had so recently committed himself at last to addressing a wider public through print. The ducal institution that now attracted him was the university of Jena, which, with the recent appointment of Johann Gottlieb Fichte (1762–1814) and of Schiller himself, had become the principal centre of Kantianism after Königsberg. Schiller's proposal of collaboration came at just the right time.

His project was very ambitious. Supported by the Stuttgart businessman Johann Friedrich Cotta (1764–1832), in whom he had at last found a publisher who believed in paying his authors well, Schiller intended to gather in all Germany's big names from its courts and universities and provide them with an outlet whose circulation would rival that of Wieland's *German Mercury*. The elite culture of the officials, the aesthetic education of which he was just writing the theory, would meet the volume market of the commercial and professional classes: the German-speaking world would have a unified literature, at once sophisticated and popular. Launched amid intense curiosity in 1795, *The Horae*, the first venture to link the names of Goethe and Schiller, was dead in the water after two years. It failed, essentially, because it closed its pages to the one thing everyone wanted to read about: politics, and especially the French Revolution. The restriction was unavoidable: had political discussion been allowed, it would have revealed the deep divergence of interests between the two wings of the middle class which the journal was trying to unite. With its failure the gap opened up anyway, and recognition

The age of idealism (1781–1832)

of it became a permanent feature of official literature: *Xenia* (*Xenien*, 1796), the collection of satirical epigrams with which Goethe and Schiller took their revenge on the commercial book market, inaugurated a tradition of critique of the bourgeois public (*Publikumsbeschimpfung*) which has lasted to the present day.

Goethe was probably not surprised by the fate of *The Horae*. At the same time, his novel *Wilhelm Meister's Years of Apprenticeship* (*Wilhelm Meisters Lehrjahre*, 1795–6) also met with a cool reception. He sensed that the future of German literature lay with the new generation inspired by the new philosophy, who, whether they admitted it or not, could not rely on a mass public to share their concerns. For a decade young intellectuals, especially those hoping for a career as servants of the state, saw the Kantian philosophical revolution as Germany's moral alternative to the French political revolution and looked to Kantianism to reinterpret or replace the religious faith that Enlightenment had shaken. *Wilhelm Meister* was written for them, though it had something more disturbingly revolutionary to teach them than they were perhaps willing to learn. Through a story of emancipation from the Storm and Stress illusion of the transformative power of literature and the theatre, it tells the deeper story of a young man's education out of the delusive belief that his life is in the hands of some external power, such as providence or fate, and into the recognition that meaning is something he has to make for himself. Goethe recognized that, however conciliatory it appeared on the surface, philosophical idealism was based on a self-assertion profoundly disruptive of our relation with our historical and natural origins, and that in that sense it was indeed part of the same revolution that was taking a political form in France. As the military consequences of the Revolution gradually engulfed Germany Goethe made repeated attempts, none of them wholly successful, to represent it directly in literature. Success came indirectly when, at Schiller's urging, he resumed work on *Faust*, of which he had published a fragmentary version in 1790. He revised and greatly extended his '*Urfaust*' draft, altering his original conception so much that he decided to divide the material into two parts, of which the first was ready for the printer by 1806. If the *Urfaust* was a transposition of an old story into a contemporary mode, *Faust. Part One* is an ironical reversion to the old story itself: Goethe multiplies the points of contact with the original legend, in particular preparing the way for Faust to conjure up Helen of Troy in *Part Two* and so reducing the affair between Faust and Gretchen to an episode. But *Part One* still ends with the tragic scenes that conclude the *Urfaust* and the target of its irony is the notion that anything as inseparable from Christian ideas as the 16th-century tale of a man who sells his soul to the devil can have any relevance to the modern world. Faust emphatically dissociates himself from the Christian past when, in a new scene showing his agreement with Mephistopheles, he commits himself to living life to the full and for its own sake and wagers that he will never find anything in the world more valuable than his own capacity for experiencing it. *Part One* is thus, in its own way, as much an updating of the myth as the *Urfaust*: its Faust represents an idealist and revolutionary era as much as his predecessor represented an era of Storm and Stress; and his catastrophic involvement with Gretchen amounts to as penetrating an interrogation of the moral foundations of modernity.

For nearly ten years after the arrival of Fichte, the university of Jena was the intellectual centre of Germany, the vortex, as Ezra Pound would have said, in which many of the philosophical, theological, sociological, and aesthetic ideas dominant in the modern world were formed. With Goethe, Herder, and Wieland nearby, Fichte and Schiller were a magnet for younger talent. The brothers Wilhelm and Alexander von Humboldt (1767–1835 and 1769–1859), key figures in 19th-century philology and natural science respectively, were both attracted. Schiller's Württemberg connections brought across three former students from the Lutheran seminary in Tübingen who between them changed the face of Western thought: the poet Friedrich Hölderlin

(1770–1843), and the two philosophers he inspired, Friedrich Wilhelm Joseph Schelling (1775–1854) and Georg Wilhelm Friedrich Hegel (1770–1831), both of whom held chairs in Jena. The translator, literary critic, and gifted versifier August Wilhelm Schlegel (1767–1845) took up residence in order to collaborate on *The Horae* and begin his verse translation of Shakespeare (completed 1823) and his brother Friedrich (1772–1829), a brilliant literary theorist and aphorist, but less sure-footed as a philosopher and novelist, soon followed. Friedrich Schlegel first gave currency to the term 'romantic' as a description of post-classical literature generally, and particularly of literature that lent itself to being understood in terms of the new idealist philosophy, as an expression or exploration of subjectivity. If any one person can be said to have founded 'Romanticism', it is he. With his brother he started a journal, *Athenaeum* (1798–1800), in which he published his own essays and 'fragments' – aphorisms and brief speculations on literary and philosophical topics – and some of the fragments and poems of his close friend Friedrich von Hardenberg, known as 'Novalis' (1772–1801). Novalis had studied in Jena and still took time away from his post as a Saxon mining official to visit it, and he provided Schlegel with a tangible example of what 'romantic' literature might be. His *Hymns to Night* (*Hymnen an die Nacht*) explicitly reversed the imagery of Enlightenment to proclaim a revival of the power of religion. But it was an idealist's religion, which explored the universe – and Novalis had a polymath curiosity about the world – as a dimension of the self: 'The way of mystery leads inwards. Within us, or nowhere, lies eternity with all its worlds'. To this total interfusion of world and self Novalis, like Schlegel, gave the name of 'poetry'. Novalis rescued religion from secularization, but at the price of making it indistinguishable from aesthetics. Schelling had no time for Novalis' medievalism (provocatively expounded in *Christendom or Europe* [*Die Christenheit oder Europa*], 1799) but, like Hölderlin and Hegel, he was impressed by Schiller's theory of aesthetic education and gave 'Art', as the subject matter of aesthetics was now called, pride of place at the summit of his

System of Transcendental Idealism (1800). In lectures he argued
that the support of 'Art' was a proper concern of the state, so
advancing 'artists' – including poets – to the rank of functionaries
like the clergy of the state church. Literature, thus understood,
was a high calling, deserving the attention of metaphysicians,
but it lost its direct link to the public, and to the market-place.
It could not take seriously the realistic stories of bourgeois life
that were currently so successful with English book-buyers. And
because it was to be written by officials, or by those aspiring to
office, it could not be written by women.

But if literature was not to be 'Art', what else could it be in a
Germany where only those close to the central state power
could have any sense of what really determined collective life
and social identity? Johann Paul Friedrich Richter, known as
'Jean Paul' (1763–1825), in what, for want of a better word, must
be called his novels, made a serious attempt to transfigure the
trivial alternative, and had a considerable commercial success,
particularly with women readers. But in order to be realistic
about the Germany that lay outside the orbit of the higher officials
he had to concentrate on lives that were crushed, distorted, or
excluded from power, and these he could make significant only
by diluting his realism with sentiment, fantasy, religiosity, and
Sternean self-irony, unfortunately without Sterne's concision. In
Titan (1800–3), he satirized the aesthetic pretensions of Weimar
society, on the margins of which he settled between 1796 and 1801.
Goethe, though, was actually rather sceptical of grand claims
for the power of poetry. He could see that the tide had turned
and that the aim of *The Horae*, to establish a republic of letters
that could unite the Germany of the courts with the Germany
of the publishers, was no longer feasible. After the treaty of
Campo Formio in 1797, the Holy Roman Empire, which provided
the political framework for the project, was clearly in terminal
decline. And as the Empire disaggregated, under pressure from
Napoleon, so the universities of the smaller states, which had
relied on the Empire as their catchment area, lost their role.

Alone, Saxe-Weimar was not big enough to contain the energies concentrated in Jena: external threats led to the sacking of Fichte, on a charge of atheism, in 1799 and thereafter the luminaries trickled away.

Goethe turned to the court: perhaps in the theatre, which so far he had treated as a sideline, he could achieve on the small scale the cultural integration which had been too much for *The Horae*. In 1798 a completely rebuilt theatre was reopened with Schiller's first new play for over a decade, *Wallenstein*, a verse tragedy in three parts, and over the next seven years Goethe deliberately tried to create a house style that could accommodate both crowd-pulling sentimental or musical entertainments and advanced intellectual experiment. The middle ground was triumphantly occupied by Schiller who had also achieved a successful compromise in his personal arrangements, maintaining his freedom by relying principally on his earnings from Cotta, but with insurance provided by his ducal stipend and by the crucial promise of a pension if his frail health should give way. Between 1800 and his death in 1805 he wrote four more major plays for Weimar, combining elements from both the Shakespearean and the French traditions, spectacular, stageable, popular, and profound. In *Wallenstein, Maria Stuart* (1800), and *The Maid of Orleans* (*Die Jungfrau von Orleans*, 1801), he tested out Kant's moral psychology in circumstances of increasing complexity, striving for the impossible goal that his aesthetic theory had put before him: to give visible and tangible manifestation to human freedom and the human power of self-redemption, which he believed persist even when most implacably opposed by political reality. In *Maria Stuart*, for example, Queen Elizabeth is physically free but morally has chosen to become the slave of external forces, while Mary Queen of Scots, though physically imprisoned, acquires a moral autonomy that frees her from the burden of past guilt. Schiller is able to represent Mary's transcendental liberation, however, only by recourse to an older symbolic language – he stages a scene of sacramental confession and communion – which

7. *A Glimpse of Greece at its Zenith* (1825) by the artist and architect Karl Friedrich Schinkel (1781–1841). The vision of a society at harmony with itself and Nature, and celebrating human and divine beauty through art, was the inspiration of the German Hellenistic, or 'classical', movement

presupposes a different source of redemption and can be seen as effectual only if it is not seen as a mere theatrical metaphor. Schiller's last completed play, *Wilhelm Tell* (1804), with its themes of collective, rather than individual, liberation, and of the justifiability of murder in a political cause, suggests that when death overtook him he was already trying to move beyond the moral confines of Kantian idealism. But in his struggle with Kant's immensely powerful analysis of subjectivity Schiller produced studies of human identity at odds with its political context which psychologically and formally are still as compellingly problematic as when he wrote them.

What Schiller made dramatic, Hölderlin made fully tragic. His odes, elegies, and Pindaric 'hymns', his novel *Hyperion* (1797–9), his unfinished drama, *The Death of Empedocles* (*Der Tod des Empedokles*, 1798–9), and his translations of Sophocles together make up one of the lonely summits of modern European literature. Hölderlin belonged to a generation of young people whose formative experience was the first flush of excitement at the outbreak of the French Revolution: a vision of the possibility of human transformation which remained with them even when the Revolution itself faded away into *Realpolitik* and imperialist wars and the hope of transplanting it into Germany was repeatedly disappointed. At the same time he and his fellow students of theology experienced the first impact of the Kantian moral philosophy. After its aesthetic reinterpretation by Schiller, they combined it with Winckelmann's Hellenism to create an image of ancient Greek religion as the liberated and humanist alternative to the joyless and authoritarian Lutheranism imparted in the seminaries. But Hölderlin had too deep an understanding of Christianity to be able to detach himself from it completely. And in 18th-century Germany there were no jobs for priests of Apollo. Schelling and Hegel broke into university philosophy but Hölderlin's attempts at an academic career were ineffectual, he could earn little from publication, and for as long as his sanity lasted, he had to earn his living as a private tutor. He finally succumbed to schizophrenia in 1806 but by then he had had the 'one summer ... and one autumn for ripe song' that he asked the fates to grant him. The poetry of his few years of maturity is marked by a uniquely powerful sense of an imminent – though never actual – divine epiphany:

Nah ist

Und schwer zu fassen der Gott.

Wo aber Gefahr ist, wächst

Das Rettende auch.

[Near is,/And hard to grasp, the God./Where though there is danger grows/The means of rescue also.]

The modernity of this sense of the divine lies partly in its historicity: in Hölderlin's conviction that God has been incarnated in human time, in the culture of Periclean Athens and in the life of Jesus Christ, and could or should have become flesh again in his own revolutionary age, possibly in a German aesthetic republic. But the modernity also lies in the overwhelming integrity of the poetry which is the vehicle of the conviction. Hölderlin summoned an objective divine presence out of the depth of his faith and remained its prophet even when it turned into divine absence. He lived by his vocation, even when it seemed to condemn him to failure and madness. The sense of exposure to an inscrutable and impersonal fate grows in his later verse but it is matched by an extraordinary fortitude that continues to trust in the power of the word, or even of single words, to catch the sunlight of meaning. His finest poems – such as *Bread and Wine* (*Brod und Wein*), *Patmos*, *Midway through Life* (*Hälfte des Lebens*) – are the supreme achievement of the Idealist age in German literature. But the achievement was dearly purchased.

(ii) The birth of nationalism (1806–32)

The course and character of German nationalism was largely
determined by Napoleon. By replacing the Holy Roman Empire
with a collection of nominally sovereign, client states he deprived
Germans of the federal identity they had possessed for centuries.
By his decision, which he came to regret, not to suppress the
kingdom of Prussia after his defeat of its armies at Jena and
Auerstädt in 1806, he virtually guaranteed that Prussia would
be the focus of any attempt to define a new unity, at least by
Protestants. The symbol of Prussia's determination to reform
itself after defeat was already a symbol of its new awareness
of its political and cultural centrality: the University of Berlin,
founded in 1810 at the instigation of Wilhelm von Humboldt,
with Fichte as its rector, clearly aspired to succeed Jena as
a university for all Germany (and both Hegel and Schelling
eventually taught there), but its location in the capital city (unique
in Germany at the time) proclaimed that the life of the mind
was henceforth fully integrated into the life of the centralized
sovereign state.

In literature the transition from the cosmopolitan idealism
of the Jena period to recognition of the determining role of
the nation-state can be traced in the career of a lonely genius.
Heinrich von Kleist (1777–1811), sprung from an illustrious
Prussian military family, was in philosophical and literary matters
self-taught. Desperate to escape his hereditary destiny to be
a soldier he tried to earn his living as a writer and journalist.
He discovered Kant for himself but, unaware of post-Kantian
developments, was more affected by Kant's critical questions
than by his constructive answers, and in his plays and stories
mounted a searing assault on the moral psychology on which
Schiller's mature work was based. In both his tragedy *Penthesilea*
(1808), for example, which shows a Greece totally lacking in the
nobility and calm that Winckelmann prized, and in his enigmatic
story *The Marchioness of O ...* (*Die Marquise von O.*, 1808), the

heroine attempts in Schillerian fashion to defy the world and rely on the certainty of her own self-knowledge, only to discover that the self is fallible. Kleist's later work, such as the story *Trial by Combat* (*Der Zweikampf*, 1811) and the drama *Prinz Friedrich von Homburg* (1809–10), begins to suggest a way out of the dilemma: after suffering a breakdown like one of Kleist's earlier figures, the Prince of Homburg recovers his identity by acknowledging that it depends on his membership of a human community, in his case the embryonic state of Prussia. The new insight came too late to save Kleist, however. Unable to make a living from his writing, and reduced to begging for any sort of an official position, he committed suicide in a pact with a woman with incurable cancer.

With the exception of Kleist, Prussian writers of the early 19th century had difficulty in establishing any organic continuity with the idealist literary culture of the small courts that had borne so much fruit in the last years of the Holy Roman Empire. It is unfortunate that the term 'Romanticism' is used to refer both to the work of Friedrich Schlegel, Schelling and Novalis in linking the new philosophy of subjectivity with ideas about 'Art', religion, and the state, and to the Prussian literature of escape that reflected the condition of the monarchy's oppressed bourgeoisie, and was in effect the emerging intellectual end of the commercial literature of entertainment. (Between 1770 and 1840 adult literacy rose from 15% to 50% of the German population, and by 1800 secular literature accounted for four times as many new titles as popular theology, so reversing a historic relationship which had held good until the middle of the 18th century.) Johann Ludwig Tieck (1773–1853), a Berliner who discovered the charms of the old Empire, residing in Jena in its great days and editing the literary remains of Novalis, followed Jean Paul as one of the first fully professional German men of letters who was not a mere hack. But he was a literary jackdaw, appropriating whatever was fashionable and could be made to sell without always appreciating its worth – his *The Wanderings*

of Franz Sternbald (*Franz Sternbalds Wanderungen*, 1798),
for example, imitated *Wilhelm Meister* while stripping out the
analysis of identity that made Goethe's novel both significant and
inaccessible. Ernst Theodor Amadeus Hoffmann (1776–1822)
was a more considerable talent, a gifted musician, a highly placed
legal official, and a true disciple of Jean Paul. He both exaggerated
his master's contrast between reality and fantasy and made it a
more explicit expression of the contrast between the corralled
bourgeoisie and the free-floating intellectuals to whom Germany
owed its new conception of culture (*Life and Opinions of Murr
the Tom-Cat* [*Lebens-Ansichten des Katers Murr*], 1820–2). The
nightmarish element in the fantasy, which he shares with Tieck,
hints none the less at the bourgeoisie's deeply buried aggression
against the bureaucratic, purportedly rational, political order (*The
Sandman* [*Der Sandmann*], 1815). Cut off by his Catholicism
from the aesthetic idealism of Weimar and Jena, which was by
origin entirely Protestant, and exiled from his Silesian homeland
to the civil service in Berlin, Joseph von Eichendorff (1788–1857)
turned a similar sense of alienation into melodious and nostalgic
poems, still widely popular, on Goethean landscapes – hills,
forests, warm summer moonlight – in which, however, the charm
of an impersonal distance is substituted for Goethe's ever-present
and ever-reactive self.

It was Fichte who found a way to link the Jena philosophy of
subjectivity with the political imperative to define German life
in terms of the new concept of the nation-state and who thus
made it possible for a unified Germany to seem a compelling
intellectual necessity. In 1807–8, in a Berlin still garrisoned by the
French, he delivered a series of *Addresses to the German Nation*
(*Reden an die deutsche Nation*) in which he claimed that idealist
philosophy necessarily gave a unique place in European history to
Germany, since Germany had given birth to idealist philosophy,
and called on Germans to identify themselves with this historical
mission by identifying themselves with the state that was its

embodiment. The apex of the conceptual pyramid, which in Jena had been occupied by Art, was in Berlin to be occupied by the historical life of the nation. A new wave of enthusiasm for the German past swept across intellectual Germany, but unlike the historical turn of the Storm and Stress years it was motivated, not by the search for cultural resources that pre-dated absolutism, but by the search for a nationhood that could be opposed to that of the occupying French. It was both more escapist and more professionally purposeful than the movement of the previous generation and was principally directed not towards the 16th century, when the federal Empire was still relatively strong and the bourgeoisie was still in the ascendant, but towards an earlier Middle Ages, and chivalrous and pious myths that disguised military and state power rather than responding to economic realities. The Prussian Ludwig Achim von Arnim (1781–1831) joined forces with Clemens Brentano (1778–1842) from Frankfurt, who was the son of an early flame of Goethe's and whose sister Arnim eventually married, to collect (mainly southwest) German folk songs as Goethe and Herder had done. But the nostalgic tone of their highly successful anthology, *The Boy's Magic Horn* (*Des Knaben Wunderhorn*, 1806–8), betrayed that it was the voice of a Germany that was a past or future, not a present reality. Serious medieval philology was already beginning, however; the *Lay of the Nibelungs* was translated in 1807 by a future professor of German literature at the University of Berlin; and the scholars Jakob and Wilhelm Grimm (1785–1863, 1786–1859) collected Hessian 'fairy' tales and launched the first historical dictionary of the German language (which took well over a hundred years to complete). The universities were, as Fichte envisaged, a focus of the more political forms of nationalism, and students – and student-poets not otherwise of literary significance – were prominent among the volunteers who, as a historical mirror-image of the French popular armies in the early Revolutionary days, and in black, red, and gold uniform, helped to sweep away the invaders in the 'Wars of Liberation' of 1812–14.

Germany's federal tradition continued, however, to be of cultural importance. While Prussia grew towards a bureaucratic model of the nation-state and Austria turned its attention south and east, the smaller German territories kept alive something of the spirit of the old Empire, its cosmopolitanism, and its belief in a literary and intellectual community larger than the local political unit. Hegel, though often misrepresented as a Prussian nationalist, saw the model of political life in the constitutional monarchies which briefly, between 1815 and the Carlsbad decrees of 1819, looked like Germany's future, and in his maturity he regarded contemporary Germany as a structure of interrelated sovereign states, not, even potentially, as a single polity. His encyclopaedic interest in world history was typical of the curiosity that could flourish in German courts and universities, uncompromised by any imperialist designs of their own, about the wider world being opened up to Europe by its newly expanding empires. Wilhelm von Humboldt and the Schlegels made themselves expert in the languages of ancient India, while Alexander von Humboldt, after years of exploration in the Americas, began to see the world as a single biological system (*Cosmos*, 1845–62). A different kind of desire to transcend incipient nationalism was shown by a number of intellectuals who converted to Catholicism and thereby opted out of official idealist culture altogether: Friedrich Schlegel, who converted in 1808, and Zacharias Werner (1768–1823), an able dramatist, whom Goethe briefly considered a possible successor to Schiller in Weimar, but who ended life as a priest in Vienna.

Goethe held his own course through these troubled waters. The death of Schiller and the battle of Jena, which nearly led to the extinction of the duchy of Weimar, were traumatically decisive events for him, and after his experiment with Werner he took a public stand against 'Romanticism' and especially Romantic religiosity. His subtle and complex novel, *Elective Affinities* (*Die Wahlverwandschaften*, 1809), based on an episode in the career of the Schlegels, structured around one of the supreme examples of the device of the unreliable narrator, and set in a country house

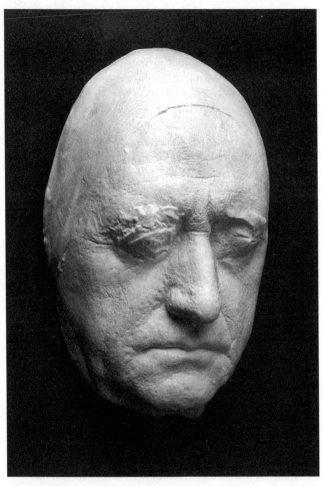

8. Life mask (1807) of Goethe at 58 – the nearest we have to a photograph of him

and parkland whose symbolic implications only gradually become apparent, shows the tragically destructive effects of Romantic attitudes on the lives and feelings of four contemporary people. Goethe also found it easier than many of his fellow Germans to reconcile himself to the rule of Napoleon, who seemed to him an almost legitimate successor to the Holy Roman Emperor and a continuator of the Enlightenment tradition of firm but rational government. In the later years of the Napoleonic Empire, he felt sufficiently at ease with himself and his public to embark on an extensive autobiography, an avowed and often misleading stylization of a literary career which he now thought was largely in the past, *Truth and Fiction from my Life* (*Aus meinem Leben Dichtung und Wahrheit*, 1811–33). But the turmoil of Napoleon's overthrow, and the reactionary and churchy atmosphere of the Restoration, isolated him once more and provoked a new outburst of poetic activity as he fled in his imagination into the sceptical, non-Christian, wine-bibbing, and erotically relaxed atmosphere of medieval Iran. *The Parliament of East and West* (*West-Östlicher Divan*, 1819), the collection of poems which he wrote in an extraordinary conversation across the centuries with the Persian poet Hafiz, found few admirers at the time – though Hegel was among them – but it anticipated an orientalizing strand in poetry which lasted for most of the 19th century. In the last third of his life, Goethe turned definitively to print as the focus of his activity and to three increasingly weighty editions of his collected works. For the last of these, intended to secure the financial future of his family, he obtained the first grant of an effective copyright for all the German-speaking territories: Germany had finally become a nation, if only in literature. But Goethe was not moved by nationalist fervour and was suspicious of the nation-state, especially Prussia. He thought of himself as writing for the like-minded, wherever they might be, and increasingly as writing for the future, reserving the publication of the second part of his life's work, *Faust*, until after his death. *Faust. Part Two* (1832) is Goethe's last word on the age he had lived through, a poetic and symbolic panorama taking in the misrule and frustrations of the last years of the *ancien régime*, the quixotic cultural endeavours of the great age of idealism (symbolized in Faust's brief marriage to Helen of Troy), the explosion of violence in revolution and war, and the advance of capital and industry, empire, and undisguised state power, in the post-Napoleonic era. Through it all Faust threads his way, his fateful wager now virtually a symbol of the moral ambivalence of modernity, as destructive as it is creative. Goethe's final judgement on Faust is correspondingly ambiguous, poised between an annihilating, but realistic, dismissal by Mephistopheles and a triumphant, but ironical, expression of hope by the hosts of heaven: a permanent challenge to us who come after to reassess the play, and ourselves.

Chapter 4
The age of materialism (1832–1914)

(i) Mind and matter (1832–72)

Between the two French revolutions of 1830 and 1848, German writers had to battle to define themselves on two different fronts. They had to resist (or accept) the repression and censorship with which their rulers sought to prevent the French contagion from spreading eastwards. And they had to accept (or repudiate) the inheritance of the great period of cultural achievement which had come to an end with the deaths of Beethoven, Hegel, and Goethe. But in this battle who was the enemy? Was it the repressive monarchy and bureaucracy, to which, after all, the great minds of two previous generations had accommodated themselves? To say that would be to align yourself with the bourgeoisie whom the age of absolutism had excluded both from political power and from significant literary activity. Or was the enemy the bourgeois themselves who, as chronic non-participants, deserved to be ridiculed as 'philistines' (a student slang term which, with the sense of 'impervious to the Art of the elite' came into general currency at this time)? That would be to cut yourself off from the class which in France and England was most obviously the instrument of economic, technological, and political modernization. It was an age therefore of reluctant bourgeois, and disaffected or failed officials, whose preferred relationship to their inheritance was to accept it but to reverse what they took to be its own understanding of its achievements.

The doubly ambivalent relationship to the past is crisply clear in the case of philosophy. The philosophers who dominated the new age in Germany were materialist where their predecessors had been idealist, and socially autonomous where their predecessors had been dependent. The new leaders of thought made their way outside the institutions of state. Arthur Schopenhauer (1788–1860) led a life of permanent semi-retirement on the proceeds of his father's commercial career, reinvested in banking concerns. Ludwig Feuerbach (1804–72) was supported for the greater part of his career by a porcelain factory owned by his wife. Karl Marx (1818–83) in his later years could rely on the assistance of Friedrich Engels' (1820–95) family money, derived from the Manchester textile industry. Friedrich Nietzsche (1844–1900) also had the support of a family inheritance originally made in England, and not forfeited when his brother-in-law was bankrupted by a bizarre colonial adventure in Paraguay. Moreover, as literacy rose, the great expansion of publishing and journalism (the number of bookshops in Berlin, Leipzig, and Stuttgart more than doubled between 1831 and 1855) gave to Marx, and especially to the radical religious writer David Friedrich Strauss (1808–74), the opportunity of being a literary freelance which had been denied to Hölderlin and Kleist. From 1830 to 1914, as neither before nor since, Germany possessed a recognizably bourgeois intellectual class, comparable with that of contemporary France and England. Recognizably bourgeois, but not always willingly so. Every one of these thinkers began with the ambition of becoming a university professor but turned away, or was prevented, from realizing it. Schopenhauer abandoned university life with relief after an unsuccessful attempt at direct competition with Hegel's lectures in Berlin, but he never forgave the academic philosophers (*Kathederphilosophen*) their popularity and their influence.

Strauss was dismissed from his teaching post in Tübingen on the publication of his deconstructive *Life of Jesus* in 1835, and the civil war (literally) that broke out in Zurich when he was proposed for the chair of theology there put him on every university's blacklist for good. In 1842, Bruno Bauer (1809–82) lost his post at Bonn for publishing critical works on the New Testament. His young protégé, Karl Marx, had in consequence to give up his academic ambitions as well and found himself launched into journalism. For years Feuerbach hoped for a chair of philosophy but had to recognize it was impossible after the publication and explosive success of his scandalous *The Essence of Christianity* (*Das Wesen des Christentums*) in 1841. Nietzsche savaged Strauss, who by the 1870s was the grand old man of German letters, but shared his scorn for the academic world, from which Nietzsche decisively alienated himself by his first publication as Basle professor of classics, *The Birth of Tragedy from the Spirit of Music* (*Die Geburt der Tragödie aus dem Geiste der Musik*, 1872). Like Schopenhauer, whom by then he also despised, Nietzsche finally retired from the university into pensioned isolation.

The philosophers of this generation did not therefore simply reject what they had inherited – dismiss it with indifference as irrelevant to a changed world. Their reaction was tinged with bitterness and pervaded by a combative desire to achieve the old aims in a new context, sometimes reluctantly chosen. It was not so much a rejection as a conscious inversion of the past. The major figures were emphatic in subordinating the human power of thought to some prior principle: in Schopenhauer the will, in Feuerbach the senses, in Marx class interest, in Nietzsche, in one form or another, all three. These very different writers had in common that they were deliberately overthrowing the primacy given to thought, or 'reason', by German philosophy from Leibniz to Hegel, and this act of regicide they all presented as a reversal of a relationship seen as prevalent in classical German philosophy. The pithiest formulation of the principle happens to stand in Marx' and Engels' *German Ideology*

(*Die deutsche Ideologie*), a manuscript of 1845–7 (published 1932), but it could as easily have been written by Schopenhauer, Feuerbach, or Nietzsche:

> It is not consciousness that determines life, but life that determines consciousness.

Since, however, it was not true that classical German philosophy thought 'consciousness determines life', the belief of its successors that they were reversing what had gone before was not true either. But the idea of a reversal had a great emotional charge for all of them and the rhetoric of inversion is everywhere in their works. As usual, behind the appearance of parricide lay feelings of love as well as of anger. The claim to reversal was really a claim to continuity, but it also expressed an angry recognition that historical change had made mere continuity impossible.

A more subtly ambivalent relation to the past runs through the literature of these years. The poetry and prose of Heinrich Heine (1797–1856) was dominated by the conviction that he had lived through the 'ending of the "Goethean aesthetic period" ' into an age of industrialism, communism, and a German revolution to come. Yet his first and most lasting success as a poet was achieved with collections of verse which seem at first sight a limpid distillation of the lyrical and folk-song manner of Goethe and, especially, *The Boy's Magic Horn* (*Book of Songs* [*Buch der Lieder*], 1827–39, *New Poems* [*Neue Gedichte*], 1844). Seen more closely, they prove to be shot through with an ironical – and Byronical – astonishment that a modern man can be such a fool as to be taken in by idealist or Romantic notions of the beauty of love, Nature, and poetry:

> Teurer Freund, du bist verliebt,
>
> Und du willst es nicht bekennen,

Und ich seh des Herzens Glut

Schon durch deine Weste brennen.

[Dear friend, you are in love and will not admit it, and I can already
see the fire in your heart glowing through your waistcoat.]

But perhaps to be modern (at any rate, in Heine's circumstances)
is to be a fool, and to live with divided loyalties. A life is no less
real, and certainly no less painful, for being divided:

Ach Gott! Im Scherz und unbewußt

Sprach ich, was ich gefühlet;

Ich hab mit dem Tod in der eignen Brust

Den sterbenden Fechter gespielet.

[Oh God, in jest, and without knowing it, I uttered what I really
felt; I played the dying gladiator with death in my own breast.]

Coming from a Jewish banking family, Heine had no love for
Restoration Germany in which, after the repeal of Napoleon's
emancipatory legislation, he had to convert to Christianity if
he was to become, as originally intended, either a lawyer or an
academic. The revolution of 1830 attracted him to Paris, and
from there he sent German newspapers reports on French art,
literature, and politics while settling accounts with his own
traditions in two pyrotechnically unflattering studies, *On the
History of Religion and Philosophy in Germany* (*Zur Geschichte
der Religion und Philosophie in Deutschland*, 1834) and *The
Romantic School* (*Die romantische Schule*, 1831–2). In 1835 the
Germanic Federation prohibited his writings, along with those of
a number of other radical authors, collectively known as 'Young
Germany' (*Junges Deutschland*). Despite the reduction in his

literary earnings Heine survived on a French state pension and occasional subsidies from his family and was able to marry his mistress, an uneducated French woman, about whom he wrote some of his warmest poems. In the 1840s, when he met the young Marx, also in exile in Paris, and contributed to his journal, his poetry turned to political satire (*Germany. A Winter's Tale* [*Deutschland. Ein Wintermärchen*], 1844: 'The Customs Union [...] will give us the "material" unity, the spiritual will be provided by the censorship office') and then to historical and Jewish themes, taking on a darker colouring.

The failure of the German 'revolution' in 1848 coincided for Heine with the onset of spinal tuberculosis which for the next eight years confined him to his bed. As he faced pain and death in this 'mattress-grave', his sense of the irony of history grew bitterly personal, but, though Heine mocks everything else, he never mocks his relationship with his audience. If his readers are involved in an absurdity – such as the attempt to see the world of waistcoats and customs unions through the spectacles of Romanticism – he ensures that they know he is involved in it too. He writes with a journalist's respect for his public, and his confidence that he has a public marks him off from the tragically isolated intellectuals and elite officials who had given him and the Germany he wrote for a literary and philosophical tradition.

> I have just come from the Christmas market. Everywhere groups of freezing children in rags standing wide-eyed and sad-faced in front of marvels made of water and flour, rubbish and tinsel. The thought that for most people even the most pitiful joys and pleasures are unattainable riches made me very bitter.

Compassion for Germany's poor and excluded drove Georg Büchner (1813–37) to an angry rejection of the tradition of idealism. He looked instead to the realism of the Storm and Stress movement that had preceded it, to Goethe's early works and the Gretchen story in *Faust*, and to the plays of Lenz. Yet his writings, most of which became known only after the publication of a collected edition in 1875, are haunted by a sense of lost wholeness and a search for the meaning of suffering that seems to require a religious answer, though it is left unformulated. In 1834 he published an insurrectionary pamphlet with the slogan 'Peace to the cottages! War on the palaces!', he was denounced to the police and in 1835 had to flee to France though he was too obscure to be named in the prohibition of Young Germany later that year. To raise money for his escape he wrote, in five weeks, a play of great originality. Thematically, *The Death of Danton* (*Dantons Tod*), owes much to Goethe's *Egmont* and Shakespeare's *Julius Caesar*, but its open form is deliberately opposed to the purposeful ethical structure of Schiller's historical tragedies and looks back to Lenz's *The Soldiers*. (The first publisher of the complete text felt he had to explain its apparent lack of structure by adding the subtitle: *Scenes from France's Reign of Terror*.) Set in March and April 1794 it draws on verbatim extracts from revolutionary speeches to show Danton drifting towards arrest, arraignment, and execution out of lethargy, complacency ('they will never dare'), disgust with the continuing pointless slaughter, and guilt over his own involvement in the September Massacres of 1792. Gradually, though, Danton recognizes that his weariness of life, his cynicism about human motives, his easy egotism, perhaps even his atheism, are all a pose and that for the sake of love he must fight to survive – but it is too late and history goes on its way. The play's language is overwrought. But its emphatically recurrent image of burial alive is justified by its essentially religious insight: that there is no escape from existence into freedom or nothingness, and that to exist is both to suffer and to love.

Büchner came of a medical family and in exile was made an anatomy lecturer in the University of Zurich. He gave up politics, but not literature. His short story, *Lenz*, which like *The Death of Danton* draws on and cites authentic materials – in this case, the diary of Pastor Oberlin, with whom Lenz stayed in 1778 –, has the complete formal assurance which the play lacks. There is no precedent in German prose, not even in Goethe or Kleist, for its dispassionate but deeply sympathetic third-person narration. In a style free from irony and artifice, the narrator voices the agony of Lenz's mental derangement but never colludes with it. Enactments of Lenz's consciousness, through metaphor or the disruption of syntax, are continuous with the cool, medical registration of his behaviour; the internal and the external are equally open to view but they are not confused:

> he could feel in himself a stirring and wriggling towards an abyss into which an implacable force was dragging him. He was now burrowing into himself. He ate little; half the nights in prayer and feverish dreams.

In a conversation with a visiting intellectual Lenz expresses his artistic principles: 'You must love humanity in order to penetrate into the particular essence of every individual'. Such love – an understanding too deep and broad to be mere identification with what is loved – is shown by Büchner in *Lenz* and in his dramatic masterpiece, *Woyzeck*. *Woyzeck* is incomplete and there is no single definitive version of it, but that hardly matters. Büchner structured the play as a series of short, discrete, strongly drawn scenes, whose effect is cumulative rather than sequential. Once again Büchner based his story on documentary material: the medical reports on a private soldier executed in 1824 for the murder of his mistress after the first plea in Germany of diminished responsibility due to insanity. Literature can have no higher aim, Büchner's Lenz says, than to reproduce a little of the life that is in God's creation, and in his Woyzeck Büchner gave life to a figure who would have been beneath the notice of all previous tragic writers, the first proletarian 'hero' in German – perhaps in any – non-comic literature. Woyzeck appears as everybody's victim, at the bottom of every hierarchy, military, social, economic, sexual; even physically he is humiliated in a fight, and he is treated as lower than a guinea-pig by the regimental doctor who uses him in his dietetic experiments. Yet he retains his humanity in the little household that he makes up with his Marie and their child, until even this is taken away from him by her adultery with the Drum-Major and in his madness he kills her. The bitter satire of Woyzeck's superiors, particularly the Doctor, the lurid scenes at a fair, a drunken parody of a sermon on man's origins in dirt, and a bleak parable of cosmic meaninglessness which sounds more like Beckett than Dickens (who began *Oliver Twist* in 1837), might seem to amount to a hopeless nihilism. But the play has a quite opposite effect. Because of its structural focus on its central character, its precision in locating his speech, and his speechlessness, in relation to the language of those around him, its insistence, against all the hierarchies that degrade and ignore him, that his suffering, and that of Marie, is worth attention, is perhaps the only thing worth attention, it is a deeply moving expression and vindication of the power of love. Büchner's death from typhus at the age of 23 robbed 19th-century Germany not just of a literary genius but of a moral genius too.

In the 1830s and 1840s the German economy was still largely agricultural, and in its rural areas and small towns, where Paris and the urban masses seemed far away, the social structures of the 18th century were little affected by the slow onset of modernity. But the growth in population, in literacy, and in the book market, was the harbinger of changes to come, and the most perceptive spirits could sense that what was making the literary life easier for them was also detaching them from the world inhabited by Goethe's contemporaries, which their outward circumstances continued to resemble. Eduard Mörike (1804–75) was educated at the Tübingen seminary as Hölderlin was, and became a Swabian country pastor, as Hölderlin might have done, though when his doubts – possibly fostered by his fellow-seminarian Strauss – became too much for him he was able, as Hölderlin was not, to become a teacher of German literature at a girl's school in Stuttgart – neither the subject nor the school (founded in 1818) existed when Hölderlin needed them. Mörike's poems, both in rhymed German and unrhymed classical metres, became widely known only towards the end of the 19th century in their settings by Hugo Wolf. With delicacy, sobriety, and gentle humour Mörike writes within the formal repertoire of Goethe, Brentano, and Eichendorff, and like them, though he also enjoys narratives and genre scenes, he favours the theme of the self in a landscape, often recognizably the landscape of southwest Germany. But Mörike's self, like Heine's, though more subtly, is divided, both against itself and from the world beyond it. It does not penetrate the landscape with symbolic meaning, not even the meaning of distance or strangeness. Instead it is self-consciously aware of its surroundings, familiar and loved though they are, as its own outer boundary, the knowable threshold of an inner mystery which cannot be known or represented. The poet drowses on a hillside in the spring sunshine, vaguely aware of warmth and light and an indefinite longing, his only distinct sensation the drone of a bee:

Mein Herz, o sage,

Was webst du für Erinnerung

In golden grüner Zweige Dämmerung?

Alte unnennbare Tage!

[O say, my heart, what memory are you weaving in the twilight of golden green branches? ('green is the golden tree of life' says Goethe's Mephistopheles to Faust) – Ancient, unnameable days!]

The unity asserted in the classical age of idealism is no more. In the age of materialism the impressions of the senses are all that can be known, and they are dissociated from a heart which is known only as the locus of unquietness and of a memory that remembers nothing.

A similar inner detachment from imagery and poetic resources which she none the less continued to use makes for the distinctive

9. *The Poor Poet* (1839) by Carl Spitzweg (1808–85), a painter of humorous scenes of middle-class life. This would-be 'Romantic' outsider, scanning his hexameters to the scheme scratched on the wall beside him, betrays his bourgeois character by his nightcap

character of the writing of Annette von Droste-Hülshoff (1797 – 1848). As a member of an established Westphalian noble family she would seem socially to belong to the *ancien régime* as much as Mörike. But she no more fitted the 18th-century model of the writer than he, though for different reasons: she was a Catholic, and a woman, the first great woman poet of modern German literature. Unlike Mörike, who seems to receive passively the mystery of experience, she fights to gain control of memory, pain, and guilt, but cannot be sure of victory. For her the ancient days may conceal an unnameable menace. Familiar images take on a quite new connotation: the distant sound of a horn in the valley recalls the lost courage of youth; the shadowy mountains before moonrise seem a sinister circle of judges. Some of the most famous motifs in poems of Goethe and Schiller – Prometheus, the lake, the cup of life cast into the waves – are reinterpreted in one of her last poems as symbols of moral nemesis. In an extraordinary – no doubt unconscious – parallel to Blake, precisely based on botanical fact, she then asks if she has to be destroyed in order that her poetry should preserve this corrective to the tradition she has inherited, as the thistle flower is consumed by the larva of the gall-fly, which reputedly has medicinal properties:

Flüstern oft hör'ich dein Würmlein klein,

Das dir heilend im Schoß mag weilen,

Ach, soll ich denn die Rose sein,

Die zernagte, um andre zu heilen?

[I often hear the whispering of that little worm of yours, that perhaps lingers healing in your womb. Alas, am I then to be the rose, gnawed apart to heal others?]

Romantic motifs – the *doppelgänger*, hints of devilry, a tree associated with both crime and retribution – run through Droste-Hülshoff's best-known prose narrative, *The Jew's Beech* (*Die Judenbuche*, 1842, not her own title). But they point not to some other level of existence but to the moral meaning of a story in which four, partly unexplained, violent deaths are shown to originate in the neglect of basic principles of humility, honesty, charity, and Catholic religious practice. The Jewish community, though treated with brutal contempt by their Christian neighbours, appear as the guardians of the moral law fundamental to Christianity but they remain mysterious and hardly knowable. Even the identity of the principal character is fractured and indeterminate. The centre of Droste's life, as of Mörike's, lies outside any world that she can depict with the literary resources she has inherited, dependent as they ultimately are on a post-Lutheran theology that equates personal identity with an omnipotent state to which she owed no allegiance.

The subjection of women to male purposes became, perhaps unwittingly, the main theme and symbol in the poetry and drama of Friedrich Hebbel (1813–63), one of the last representatives of aesthetic idealism trying to give voice to the new spirit of social and material determinism, who was supported through his early struggle to write his way out of poverty by a mistress whom he discarded, and then by his wife, one of the foremost actresses in Vienna. *Maria Magdalena* (1844), Hebbel's only drama with a contemporary setting, captures the transformation of small-town Germany as literacy spreads and urbanization begins, but *mores* are not changing fast enough to save an unmarried mother-to-be from committing suicide for fear of scandal. 'I don't understand the world any more' her bear of a father confesses in the last line of a play which anticipates the social drama of a later age and had a great success in Germany's many theatres. Hebbel had met Heine and the German communists in Paris, but politically he inclined to Hegelian constitutional monarchism. After the crisis of 1848 his reflections on the changing world became more explicitly and systematically a continuation of Hegel's theologically tinged philosophy of history, but the women remained the victims. In *Agnes Bernauer* (1852), a woman who, through no fault of her own, has become a *casus belli* is sacrificed for the greater good of the people. *Agnes Bernauer* appealed equally to the radicals of 1848, who liked the speeches of revolutionary protest, and to the conservatives, who liked the counter-affirmation of reason of state. But it was reason of state that had the last word, despite the statesman's crocodile tears: Hebbel had again caught the mood of an age, the new age of nation-building (*Gründerzeit*), in which unscrupulousness, whether political or economic, was elevated to a moral principle. 'Only one thing is necessary', he had once written to his mistress, '– that the world should exist; how individuals fare in it is a matter of indifference'.

In his last years, at the height of his fame, Hebbel met the ageing Schopenhauer and discovered in his combination of relentless determinism with outrage at the scandal of universal suffering a philosophy that matched his own long-held convictions. Hebbel was not alone in his discovery. In the 1850s, after decades of neglect, a Schopenhauer revival began among German intellectuals, while Hegelianism waned, or metamorphosed into Marxism. Schopenhauer's rejection of all historical and social theorizing appealed to the individualism encouraged by Germany's most sustained period of liberal economic expansion. However, his belief that Art was – short of annihilation – the only possible redemption of a material world totally enslaved to the cruel logic of cause and effect also offered comfort to those who had reservations about the process by which they or others were enriching themselves, but who did not want to give up the riches.

But not everyone wanted to be comforted, or to be tied like Hebbel to the philosophy and aesthetics of an earlier and less affluent age. Between 1848 and the proclamation of the Second German Empire in 1871 the German bourgeoisie finally emerged from the shadow of German officialdom and, full of the confidence of new money and prestige, threw off the leading-strings of the inherited culture. In 1855 Ludwig Büchner (1824–99) published a hugely successful summary of the new science, *Energy and Matter* (*Kraft und Stoff*), which dismissed as turgid nonsense the entire edifice of idealist philosophy. With none of the theological and ethical subtlety, or literary sensitivity, of his elder brother, Georg (whose literary remains he had edited), Büchner, the Richard Dawkins of his day, asserted the eternity of matter, the development of life out of inorganic particles, and of human beings out of lower animals, and the unscientific redundancy of any such hypotheses as God or immortality. Gone were the anguished compromises on which a hundred years of literature and philosophy had been built. True, *Energy and Matter* cost Büchner his chair in Tübingen, but as a medical practitioner and prolific journalist he could afford to enjoy independence. After the publication of *The Origin of*

Species in 1859, Büchner became an earnest propagator of the Darwinian ideas that were thought to validate the free-market principles of which they were an expression. The work of Wilhelm Busch (1832–1908), commercially one of the most successful of German poets, was Darwinian too in its way. A freelance artist and draughtsman of genius, Busch took up the format of Heinrich Hoffmann's *Struwwelpeter* (1846) and combined a telling economy of line with equally lethal epigrammatic couplets in a series of early comic strips (e.g. *Max and Moritz*, 1865). Busch's satires on pretentious poets, religious hypocrites, and the nastiness of little boys, in an amoral world where only the fittest survive, have become part of German folk memory.

The economic basis of the new intellectual freedom was the theme of another great publishing success of 1855, *Debit and Credit* (*Soll und Haben*) by Gustav Freytag (1816–95), which remained the bestselling German novel until the end of the century. Set in Freytag's homeland, Silesia, by then one of the power-houses of Prussian industry, it follows the lives of two school contemporaries, both bourgeois, both in conflict with the aristocracy, both out to make their fortune, one honest, upright, and hard-working, the other deceitful, usurious, and Jewish. The anti-Semitism – of which this is the first clearly non-religious example in German literature – is a consequence of the economic and social revolution that made the book possible in the first place. As Germany's Jews came out of their ghettoes their most lasting disability remained, by law or in practice, the prohibition on their employment by the state (including the central institution of traditional German culture, the university). They therefore came to represent in the collective psyche a pure form of the forces combining to challenge the dominance of officialdom in German political and cultural life: money, business, and *laissez-faire*. In the great 19th-century upheaval, hostility to Jews expressed the German bourgeoisie's fear of itself, of its power to destroy the autocratic and bureaucratic state which had

Die Tante kommt aus ihrer Tür;
„Ei!" – spricht sie – „Welch ein gutes Tier!"

Kaum ist das Wort dem Mund entflohn.
Schnapp! hat er ihren Finger schon.

10. Wilhelm Busch: scenes from *Hans Huckebein* (1867), the story of a malevolent raven. The text reads: 'Auntie comes out of her door. "Oh, my", she says, "what a nice creature". Scarcely have the words left her mouth when – snap! – he's got her finger'

given it its (subordinate) identity for over 300 years. Because the hostility was fundamentally an irrational self-hatred (the two main characters in *Debit and Credit* have the *same* background) it tended from the start to take on grotesque or nightmarish qualities, though in 1855 the true nightmare still lay in the distant future.

If the image of 'the Jew' was a representation of the German bourgeois as the enemy of the German official, a counter-image of the two as identical was provided in the *Gründerzeit* by the new concept of the '*Bildungsbürger*' – the citizen of the new Germany who was defined as middle class not by his economic role but by his (rather than her) education or culture. In 1867, a year after the Seven Weeks War had finally excluded Austria from the political definition of Germany, the cultural nation received legal recognition when the copyright which now secured the livelihood of contemporary writers was abolished in respect of a dozen 'classical' German authors – Goethe foremost among them – whose works were held to be so important that all publishers should be free to distribute them. Although Goethe's private papers were still inaccessible, a vast new field was thereby opened up for the universities. As independent writing became a sustainable commercial activity, the bureaucracy withdrew into the editing and philological study of the national literature. In 1872, after Bismarck had united the German states in a war against France and left them no alternative but accession to his new Empire, David Friedrich Strauss, first a critic of Bismarck but now an enthusiastic supporter, proposed that the cultivation of 'our great poets' (Lessing, Goethe, and Schiller) and 'our great musicians' (Haydn, Mozart, and Beethoven) had more value for the new Germany than a Christianity that was both incredible and obsolete. In *The Old Faith and the New* (*Der alte und der neue Glaube*), he argued that the historical basis of Christianity had been destroyed by his own researches and that its philosophical claims were refuted by modern science, particularly astronomy and Darwinian biology. What remained of spiritual needs could be satisfied in 'Art'. Strauss uttered with lumbering frankness the truth about the accommodation between the bourgeoisie and the state in the newly united Germany: that with the passing of the princes national 'culture' had now taken the place of Lutheran religion.

If there was any single contemporary who embodied modern German culture as Strauss understood it, it was Richard Wagner (1813–83), whose operas (rather than the plays of Hebbel) were the true successors to Schiller's drama and the true fulfilment of the 18th century's dream of a German national theatre. Wagner himself saw his work as the crowning synthesis of German literature, philosophy, and music, and he brought together in his personal career most of the contradictory elements that Bismarck had fused into a nation. In his twenties Wagner was closely associated with the Young Germany movement, and in his unhappy apprenticeship years in Paris from 1839 to 1842 he made the acquaintance of Heine and the Russian anarchist Bakunin, of the socialist ideas of Marx and Proudhon, and of Feuerbach's radical secularization of religion. While conductor at the Dresden opera-house in the 1840s he wrote revolutionary journalism and in 1849 took an active part in the unsuccessful local uprising. Exiled to Switzerland for the next 16 years by fear of the German police and of his creditors he gave up politics and even, for a while, composing, in favour of the written word. Drawing on his German predecessors from Winckelmann to Romanticism, who had seen the perfection of Greek art as expressing the perfection of Greek society, and modern art as the means of educating and transforming modern society, he elaborated a theory of opera as the successor to Greek tragedy and the true instrument of social revolution. In 1853 he published his libretto, in pseudo-archaic alliterative verse, of an operatic tetralogy, *The Ring of the Nibelung* (*Der Ring des Nibelungen*) – drawing more on Norse than on German material – which represented the development of society in terms of a much modified Hegelianism: from an initial fall away from a state of nature into institutions of power and property, through the growth of individualism and so of the counter-power of love, which, however, increasingly engenders conflicts of its own, until it makes all things new in the conflagration of universal revolution. Wagner's composition of the score for this colossal project was interrupted in 1854, however, by his discovery of the philosophy of Schopenhauer, which completed his conversion from political radicalism by its demonstration of the metaphysical priority of 'Art' over society, and of music over all other arts. He turned therefore to *Tristan and Isolde* (completed 1860), which shows individuals as transient, suffering manifestations of the endlessly yearning Will, and then to an opera about opera, or at least about words and music, *The Mastersingers of Nuremberg* (written 1861–7). Hans Sachs here appears as a Schopenhauerian philosopher-artist (Wagner?) whose wise guidance brings together the two lovers, Walther von Stolzing and Eva Pogner. He thus reconciles the nobility, represented by the initially arrogant (*stolz*) Walther, with the stubbornly bourgeois artisans of Nuremberg, into whose guild Walther has sought admittance. All parties can then join Sachs in his final hymn of praise to the 'sacred German art', presumably of opera, which is said to be a surer bond of national unity even than the German Empire. The union of Walther with the burghers of Nuremberg precisely parallels the union Bismarck achieved in the course of the 1860s between an autocratic and hierarchical state structure and the newly wealthy middle classes, weaned away from the parliamentarianism of 1848. It also paralleled the fairy-tale turn taken by Wagner's own life in 1864 when Ludwig II, the 19-year-old king of Bavaria, announced his intention of freeing Wagner of all practical worries and enabling him to concentrate on composition, so transforming the self-made, and nearly self-ruined, artist into a state institution.

The Ring was completed (with a Schopenhauerian inflection of the conclusion into universal pessimism), but Wagner's last 18 years became a weirdly anachronistic reprise of Goethe's time in Weimar as favourite of a minor monarch in a pre-revolutionary

11. Ludwig II's Wagnerian dream-world under construction at Neuschwanstein in the 1870s

age. That, however, was only the mirror-image of the role Strauss
had equally weirdly assigned to the literary and musical culture
of late 18th-century agricultural and absolutist Germany and
Austria: to provide spiritual sustenance to an industrial, urban,
late 19th-century mass society too modern for religion. The
incongruity between the circumstances in which this literature
and music had been produced and the purposes which they were
now expected to serve, like the incongruity between Wagner's
apparently medieval themes (which were what appealed to
King Ludwig) and the hyper-modernity of his music, could be
concealed by dubbing them 'classical', 'timeless', or 'sacred' 'Art'.
As such they could in turn conceal the incongruous hybridity of
the '*Bildungsbürger*' who consumed them, the middle classes
of the new nation, united only by 'culture'. Ludwig's patronage
allowed Wagner to build a temple to sacred German art, the opera
house at Bayreuth, which was inaugurated in 1876 with the first
complete performance of *The Ring*. To 'consecrate' (his own word)
his temple, Wagner then wrote his last opera *Parsifal* (1882) in
which Christian symbols and rituals, their original function being
explicitly declared to be obsolete, are deployed in the service of
Schopenhauer's ethics. Strauss's favourite composer was Haydn,
and he thought Schopenhauer 'unhealthy', but in *Parsifal* his
programme for a new faith for modern Germany was fulfilled.

(ii) 'Power protecting interiority' (1872–1914)

'It can only be a confusion to speak of a victory of German
"Bildung" and culture', Nietzsche wrote in the middle of the
nationalist euphoria that followed on the Franco-Prussian War
and the proclamation of Bismarck's Empire, 'a confusion that
rests on the fact that in Germany the pure concept of culture
has been lost'. In the military victory he saw rather the potential
for 'the defeat, indeed the extirpation, of the German spirit
("Geist") in favour of the German Empire'. 'Culture' for Nietzsche
required 'unity of artistic style in all the expressions of a people's
life' and German culture he saw as hopelessly disharmonious,

though he did not recognize that this disharmony resulted from forcing together the commercially successful literature and materialist philosophy of the new bourgeoisie with the elitist and idealist inheritance of the old bureaucracy. Nietzsche's was the bitterest, though not the last, expression of the resentment of Germany's cultural officials at being cheated of power by the rise of capital (*ressentiment* was the term he later made his own for the emotional revenge of history's losers on those who conquered them). In the ideal society he envisaged in *The Antichrist* (1888, published 1895), one of the last works he wrote before collapsing into incurable insanity, the dominant class, superior even to the king and the military, are the intellectuals, '*die geistigsten Menschen*'. His matchless powers of destructive, and self-destructive, criticism were directed at any attempt to reconcile the principles which underlay Germany's new success – determinist science, mass production, competitive economic individualism – with the secularized theology that had been the basis of old Germany's culture. Sometimes he criticized the old – its enlightened rationalism, its humanitarianism, and especially its more overtly religious survivals – in the name of the new. Sometimes he criticized the new – its egalitarianism, socialism, feminism, anti-Semitism – from the standpoint of the old, and now dispossessed, elite. The detachment of thought from any real social object or context became the purpose of his writing and of his solitary, wandering way of life. From any contemporary who might have seemed to personify what he stood for he distanced himself in an often violent act of self-redefinition: Strauss earned Nietzsche's virulent hostility through being a more effective critic of religion than he was; Schopenhauer, whose metaphysics were the foundation on which *The Birth of Tragedy* was built, and Wagner whose music-dramas it represented as the summit of modern culture, were later rejected for the crypto-Christianity of their ethics. Nietzsche was incapable of constructing a book-length, or even an essay-length, argument and his attempt at a *magnum opus*, his biblical pastiche, *Thus Spake Zarathustra* (*Also sprach Zarathustra*,

1883–5) suffers from the stylistic inauthenticity that he diagnosed in his contemporaries. But in his collections of aphorisms and short reflections – the best are probably *Human, All Too Human* (*Menschliches Allzumenschliches*, 1878–80) and *Beyond Good and Evil* (*Jenseits von Gut und Böse*, 1886) – Nietzsche's brilliance could show itself untrammelled by any need for sustained coherence and he became one of the most variously and subversively fruitful thinkers for the 20th century:

> 'Knowledge for its own sake' – that is the final snare that morality lays: with that you are completely entangled in it once again.

> 'I did that', says my memory. 'I cannot have done that' – says my pride, and is implacable. Eventually – memory gives in.

> He who fights with monsters should take care that he does not turn into a monster himself. And if you look long into an abyss, the abyss too will look into you.

In 1885 the Empire on which Nietzsche had declared intellectual war won one of its greatest victories. Goethe's papers were opened to the nation, on the death of his last grandchild, and Weimar became once again the city of Goethe and Schiller. A network of Goethe Societies, centred on Weimar, sprang up around Germany and the world, the houses of the poets were turned into museums, their papers were transferred into a purpose-built archive, and professors and their assistants immediately began to labour on a historical-critical edition of Goethe's works which eventually ran to over 150 volumes and was not completed until 1919. The writings of Goethe and his fellow 'classics', and the scholarship of the academic bureaucracy which edited them all, became the twin pillars of a German national literature, the common property, and tribal totem, of both wings of the '*Bildungsbürgertum*' and of the new political nation that held that strange class together. Praised or damned or played off one against the other they have retained that status in all subsequent Germanies down to the present day.

12. Nietzsche (right) and his friend, Paul Rée, rivals for the affection of Lou Andreas-Salome (left, with whip), later to have relations with Sigmund Freud and the poet R. M. Rilke. The scene was staged by Nietzsche in 1882, and entitled by him 'The Holy Trinity'

Even as the process of institutionalization was beginning, Nietzsche pointed to the false premiss on which it was based: that the 'classics' defined in 1867 were finders and builders of a national culture, when in reality they were seekers for a culture who sought in vain. In 1896, however, Nietzsche's sister moved her now famous but slowly dying brother to Weimar with all his papers, and in 1953 these literary remains of another 'classic' were finally interred in the Goethe-Schiller Archive.

Nietzsche's revulsion from the hybrid culture of Bismarck's Reich was shared, notably in Munich, the capital of the largest and most reluctant new member of the Empire. The patronage of the Bavarian kings extended beyond Wagner to a group of mostly second-rate writers and poets who saw themselves as keeping alive the spirit of aesthetic idealism in a hostile age – bourgeois men of means who did not have the courage of the materialism proper to their class and took refuge in the Art they owed to Germany's officials. Among them Paul Heyse (1830–1914), eventually a Nobel prizewinner, contributed more by a single idea than by his over a hundred works of fiction. With his anthology, *A German Treasury of Tales* (*Deutscher Novellenschatz*, 1871), and the theoretical musings that accompanied it, he created a literary concept that had the necessary multivalency to appeal to both the commercial and the academic factions in the cultural life of the Second Empire. *Novella* (*Novelle* in German) was a long-established term for a short story in prose, and there had already been some speculation (for example, by Tieck) about the characteristics of the genre. But Heyse created the idea of the 'Novelle' as a prose form which, by its consciously self-enclosed structure and symbolic coherence, could bring the undisciplined energies of realistic narrative, springing up all over Europe and reflecting the lives and concerns of a mass readership, under the control of the German concept of 'Art'. If late 18th-century poetic drama had been elite culture morphing into the book, the late 19th-century 'Novelle' was the book morphing into elite culture. 'Sister of the drama' the 'Novelle' was called by one of its most serious practitioners,

the North German lyrical poet (and state official) Theodor Storm
(1817–88) for whom isolation in Schleswig-Holstein was his own
form of protest against the new order.

Throughout the Second Empire Munich remained the centre of
the aesthetic opposition to the Prussian commercial and industrial
powerhouse that stretched from Silesia to the Ruhr. Southern,
Catholic, within reach of the Alpine passes to the Mediterranean
lands, and blessed both with a largely functionless monarchy
happy to build temples to art and music and with a stock of cheap
apartments, vacated by those who had gone to seek their fortune
in the North, it was a magnet for writers, painters, anarchists,
and secular prophets. In Munich, the fantasy could be maintained
that the combination of Hellenism and idealism achieved by
poets and philosophers in Goethe's lifetime represented a true
Germany opposed to the economic and political forces that
had in fact brought the nation into being. 'Munich is the only
city on the earth without "the bourgeois"', wrote Stefan George
(1868– 1933) '... a thousand times better than [the] Berlin
mish-mash of petty bureaucrats jews and whores.' George, a
Rhinelander who lived on private means inherited from his
bourgeois parents, originally wanted to be a Catholic priest, but
instead founded his own religion of poetry and male friendship.
Having met Verlaine and Mallarmé in Paris, he tried to give his
German verse the qualities and even (by the elimination of capital
letters) the physical appearance of French. Cultivating elusiveness,
George moved from house to house of his acquaintances, but for
a while in the 1890s he settled in Munich where he could be seen
'striding' through the cafés, 'like a bishop through the middle of
Saint Peter's'. In his privately circulated journal *Leaves for Art*
(*Blätter für die Kunst*), printed on choice paper, with carefully
selected coloured inks, and decorated with Art Nouveau vignettes
and calligraphy and the Indian mystical symbol of the swastika, he
published poems marked by esoteric content, exquisite purity of
diction, and an unfailing perfection of rhyme. *The Year of the Soul*
(*Das Jahr der Seele*, 1895) – a title taken from Hölderlin whom

George, like Nietzsche, saw as a personification of the nobility of German poetry, disregarded by Germany itself – recounts, in a progression through the seasons, the failure of love for a woman and the 'new adventure' of love for a man. George ruthlessly terminates the compromises of Mörike and Droste-Hülshoff. In his poems, the self is not so much unknowable as absent: they focus, with commanding single-mindedness, on a 'you' (*du*) who has no features of his own beyond the shared experience of the symbolic landscape, which in turn is more of an erotic dreamscape. Poetry has become the vehicle of a pure will to power, untrammelled by the opposition of independent personalities or a material world. After the turn of the century, as nationalism intensified but materialism showed no signs of losing its grip, George's writing took on a more prophetic and apocalyptic tone (*The Seventh Ring* [*Der Siebente Ring*], 1907). He devoted himself to building a circle of disciples who would look up to him as 'the Master' and would establish a spiritual kingdom within a world whose corruption, he now felt, could be cleansed only by war (*The Star of the Covenant* [*Der Stern des Bundes*], 1914).

13. Title spread of the first edition of *The Seventh Ring* (1907) by Stefan George; design by Melchior Lechter (1865–1937)

If in the Second Empire Munich was the capital of Art, Berlin was the capital of Reality. In rapidly expanding Berlin Germany at last had the context and opportunity for a metropolitan and realist literature, to compare with that of 19th-century Paris, London, or St Petersburg. There is nothing reluctant or unsophisticated about the modernity of Theodor Fontane (1810–1989), a professional journalist and poet, who after periods of residence in England and France settled in Berlin and wrote 14 novels about the new Prussia in the last 20 years of his life. During the 1880s, Fontane advanced from historical themes to the life of his own time. *Comedies of Errors* (*Irrungen, Wirrungen*, 1888), so concise it could be called a *Novelle*, is the first masterpiece of his mature style which, with its rich texture of unobtrusive leitmotifs and its plot largely driven forward by the apparent contingencies of closely observed conversation, suggests the contemporary manner of the much younger Henry James. If the central theme – the doomed love between Botho, a nobleman, and Lene, a woman of the lower middle class – seems to hark back to mid-18th-century literature, to *Intrigue and Love*, and Storm and Stress, that reflects the historical significance of Fontane's achievement. As a pronounced Anglophile he had recovered the ambition of those earlier, and defeated, revolutionaries to create a German equivalent to the English novel of contemporary society, and he was fulfilling it. The class difference that separates the lovers, and the political repression that sustains it, are symbolized in Lene's inability to understand the English inscriptions on two pictures – which otherwise appeal to her – on the wall of the hotel room where she and Botho are happy together, two icons of the Anglo-Saxon tradition of resistance to autocracy: 'Washington crossing the Delaware' and 'The last hour at Trafalgar'. England, and a reminiscence of Trafalgar, in the person of a visiting Mr Nelson, also provide a measure of Germany's internal discords in *Frau Jenny Treibel* (1893), which is devoted to the comic discrepancy between the two forms of the '*Bildungsbürger*', the bourgeois and the academic. But Fontane was more than a satirist, he was a moralist with a penetrating sense of political and historical realities. He could not be content with merely criticizing his society: he had to use the representation of it to reflect on ultimate questions of right and wrong and human purpose. In 1892 he began a series of novels which achieve something almost without precedent in German literature: presenting lives which are as independent, responsible, and free of political oppression as it is possible for human lives to be, because they are lived by members of a ruling class. In *Beyond Recall* (*Unwiederbringlich*, 1892), *Effi Briest* (1895), and *Der Stechlin* (1898), Fontane did what his 18th-century predecessors were unable to do. He brought the resources of literary realism to bear on a class which was its own master: the landowning Prussian nobility, for the sake of which Bismarck had constructed his Empire, and which was charged by him with restraining the political ambitions of Germany's bourgeoisie. But the issues of meaning and conscience, of deeds and consequences and the passing of time, that Fontane's characters have to face transcend their historical circumstances and they know it. *Effi Briest* in particular stands out for the tautness of its psychological and symbolic structure. It is not just about the drift into adultery of its lively heroine, caught in a loveless marriage to an older husband, ambitiously climbing the ladder of promotion in one of Bismarck's ministries, but about the consequences of the accidental discovery of the adultery years later. Effi's husband, von Innstetten, allows himself to be constrained by the code of honour of his caste to kill his rival in a duel, to divorce his wife, and to separate her from her only daughter, thus destroying four lives, including his own. Why he does this, he does not know, and neither do we. Is there in him a streak of cruelty? Does he just lack the human sympathy of the novel's narrator, or of Effi's faithful Catholic maidservant, or even of her dog? Or is he a victim of some fate greater than himself, as unavoidable as social existence yet as arbitrary as the seeming chance that we live in one time rather than another? 'You *are* right!' says the friend in whom Innstetten confides. 'The world just is the way it is, and things don't happen the way we want but the way *other* people want ... Our cult of honour is idolatry, but we have to submit to it as long as the idol is believed in.' Because von Innstetten belongs to the class of those who have power, the compulsion to which he and the other characters think they have to submit is shown to us as something whose form might change with a redistribution of power but which would not then itself be eliminated. In bowing to it they are not deluded, and their human worth depends on the spirit in which they perform the obligations imposed by their transient but inescapable time and place. And so they seem proper objects of the narrator's tactful and understated compassion as well as of his irony. Fontane knew intimately the class he made central to his three greatest novels, but he did not himself belong to it. His realism therefore always hints at another perspective from that of his principals, at the historical certainty that one day the insubstantial pageant will all fade and another idol in another temple demand submission. 'Our old families are all victims of the idea that "things won't work without them", which is quite wrong', says a thoughtful character in Fontane's last novel, *Stechlin*. 'Wherever we look we are in a world of democratic attitudes. A new age is dawning.'

In the new century the old Prussian families, and Prussia itself, did indeed pass away. For Berlin's younger generation of writers they were already an irrelevance in a technological and industrial age. Literature needed to concentrate not on the landed but on the monied classes, and on those out of whom they made their money, the new class of industrial workers. The Naturalist movement of the 1880s and 1890s, led by Arno Holz (1863–1929) and Johannes Schlaf (1862–1944), was partly an enthusiastic response to the work of Zola and Ibsen, but it was also a recovery of the native German tradition of radical bourgeois realism which had last surfaced in the mid-18th century and then in the work of Büchner (whose *Woyzeck*, its title mistranscribed as *Wozzeck*, was first published in 1878). To that extent its aims were allied to those of Fontane, who reviewed some of its productions favourably. The affluence that made it possible to live as a professional novelist had a similar effect on drama, particularly since princely Germany continued to maintain the extensive network of subsidized theatres. Censorship might be strict, but in a centre of wealth such as Berlin it could be evaded. The impresario Otto Brahm (1856–1912) founded a private (and so uncensored) theatre club, where the first production, in 1889, was of Ibsen's *Ghosts*, banned for its discussion of syphilis, and the second the even more scandalous *Before Sunrise* (*Vor Sonnenaufgang*), the first mature work of Gerhart Hauptmann (1862–1946), on the theme of hereditary alcoholism (a typical fantasy of the age of eugenics). Hauptmann, a Silesian who, supported at first by his wife, took up a writing career in Berlin, had like Heine an ambiguous attitude to the modern age which he was introducing into literature: in an early poem about a train journey by night his reverie occasioned by the moonlit landscape outside the carriage is interrupted by thoughts of the impoverished and angry workers who built the line for his comfort. Inspired not by theory but by a hugely generous sympathy, he was willing for a while to be dubbed a Naturalist by Holz and Schlaf, but it was not long before he showed the more subjective side of his versatile talent.

The family devastated by drink in *Before Sunrise* is an archetype of Bismarck's Germany: Silesian farmers transformed overnight by mineral wealth into industrial capitalists. Into their brutish milieu intrudes a journalist full of the materialist and determinist ideas of the time, who seems to their Werther-reading daughter to offer a hope of escape. But as a good Darwinian he cannot bring himself to marry her for fear of the family's supposed hereditary taint and, like Werther, she kills herself. The weak-willed intellectual, a lineal descendant of the theologian with doubts to whom 18th-century literature owed so much, is a constant feature of Hauptmann's works with a contemporary setting. The figure personifies Hauptmann's reluctance to follow Fontane and extend the scope of his realism to the classes which were the locus of political power: a passive acceptance of necessity can be made to

14. Emil Orlik (1870–1932): poster for a performance of *The Weavers* in 1897

seem an adequate response to suffering if you do not include in the world you represent people who are free to act.

Disguised, such a spokesman for myopia even appears in Hauptmann's masterpiece *The Weavers* (*Die Weber*, 1892). *The Weavers* is a triumph of the manner pioneered by the young Goethe, Lenz, and Büchner, a drama with many strands and no hero, which lives from the energy of the language of the workers (Hauptmann first drafted it in his native dialect). Its theme, the uprising of the starving Silesian cottage-weavers against the factory owners in 1844 and its suppression by military force, led to repeated attempts to prohibit its performance (and the new Emperor, Wilhelm II, cancelled his subscription to Brahm's theatre in disgust). But, as Fontane remarked in his review, it is a revolutionary play with an anti-revolutionary conclusion. In the last act an elderly weaver emerges as the play's moral centre, urging non-violence, and is killed in the closing moments by a stray bullet. Fontane tellingly pointed to the parallels with

Schiller. Unlike the novel, the drama was in Germany still too implicated in the princely past to reflect the realities of power in the new society. Hauptmann revived not only the realism of Lenz's era but its self-emasculating submission to autocracy and eventually its diversion into idealism. In 1896, his five act 'fairy drama', *The Sunken Bell* (*Die versunkene Glocke*) showed he was himself still an obstinate dreamer in the moonlight. In 1912 he received the Nobel Prize for Literature.

Looking back on the career of Richard Wagner in 1933, Thomas Mann (1875–1955) saw in it the typical progression of the entire German middle class from the disappointed revolution of 1848 to resigned cultivation of 'interiority protected by power' (*machtgeschützte Innerlichkeit*) in Bismarck's Empire: an inner world of art and culture could flourish provided the authoritarian, and ultimately military, structure that protected it was not questioned. Mann was clearly thinking of himself as much as of Wagner. Few writers were as typical as he of the Second Empire middle class: in his own person he united both the bourgeoisie and the intellectuals, both Berlin and Munich. His family circumstances could not have been more bourgeois: born in what had until 1871 been the Free City of Lübeck, he was the son of a wealthy corn-merchant who married a colonial German Brazilian. After his father's death in 1891 he lived on inherited money and, later, his literary earnings: he was never, even indirectly, dependent on the state. Yet all his work was, more or less overtly, dominated by the concept of disinterested Art, the centrepiece in the ideology of 18th and 19th-century officialdom, and the bridge between the two wings of the '*Bildungsbürgertum*'. In the early 1890s the Mann family moved to Munich where, following in the footsteps of his older brother Heinrich (1871–1950), Thomas began to make a name for himself as a writer of unashamedly cynical short stories. Looking back from this new perspective on the world in which he had grown up he had his first great success with the novel *Buddenbrooks*, begun when he was only 22.

Buddenbrooks. Decline of a Family (*Buddenbrooks. Verfall einer Familie*, 1901) is Germany's greatest, perhaps only, contribution to the European 19th-century tradition of the realistic novel of bourgeois life. Its greatness, and its European status, is partly due to its being a specifically German contribution. Not just because it tells the story of four generations of a commercial family in Lübeck from 1835 to 1877, against a densely visualized backcloth of North German domestic architecture, dinner parties, and linguistic habits, of holidays by the North Sea, of schoolroom practices some of which still survive, of the strangely transient impact of public events in 1848 and the advent of street lighting. That gives a specifically German cast to the marriages, divorces, and love-affairs, the black sheep and the gossip, the social friction with commercial rivals and the deals that go awry which mark the decline of the Buddenbrook firm and the eventual extinction of the family's male line. But what makes *Buddenbrooks* more than just Galsworthy or Arnold Bennett in a German setting is a feature of its structure that only Germany could provide. Beneath the comedy, tragedy, and irony of individual lives sacrificed on the altar of the family business there is the implication of the working out of some more general principle or destiny. We seem to be pointed towards Nietzsche's critique of Schopenhauer, and his variant of the Darwinists' theory of degeneracy, of which Hauptmann had made cruder use in *Before Sunrise*. In Nietzsche's view – at times at least – the intellectual and artistic insight which for Schopenhauer offered some escape from the hideous struggle for existence was itself a symptom of failure in the struggle. As the Buddenbrook family decays, so ethical qualms, philosophical puzzlement, and artistic sensibility gain more of a hold over its will to survive. But these hints of a philosophical meaning or substructure to the story have a double effect. They open up, it is true, the possibility that the book should be read as showing that human lives are ineluctably determined and ultimately meaningless. But by raising the question of the eternal value, or valuelessness, of the characters' lives they make those lives into more than just sad or comic examples of the distortion of humanity by the power of money or social conformism: the characters and their gestures towards freedom and significance, however doomed or feeble, acquire an importance – one might call it a religious importance – which it transcends the capacity of their milieu to express. By thus uniting the novelistic realism of the European bourgeoisie with the philosophical introspection of the German official tradition Thomas Mann provided the Second Empire with its greatest literary monument. There is a price. *Buddenbrooks* is Germany without Prussia, and without the universities. Mann's early narratives (unlike the last works of Fontane, their virtual contemporary) give us society without the state. The social and economic origins of moral and personal judgements are shown, but not of the notions of 'art' and 'spirit', 'life', and 'will', which underpin the novel, and especially the short stories.

The supposed opposition between 'life' and 'art', 'the bourgeois' and 'the artist', is central to the stories Mann wrote in the next phase of his career, notably *Tristan* and *Tonio Kröger* (1903) and *Death in Venice* (*Der Tod in Venedig*, 1912). The opposition was unreal in so far as both 'bourgeois' and 'artist' were '*Bildungsbürger*', but it could appear as a real and deep opposition of metaphysical principles in so far as Mann's writing left unrepresented the ruling, 'protective' power that unified the disparate elements of German society in the service of the new German state. Instead, the unifying principle in these early narratives was Mann's writing itself. Tonio Kröger, though he becomes an 'artist' in Munich, remains in love with the North German 'bourgeois' world he has left, even when it treats him with indifference or suspicion. 'You are a bourgeois who has lost his way', a friend tells him. But he replies: 'If anything is capable of making a *littérateur* [i.e. one who writes for money] into a poet ['Dichter', i.e. one who writes out of dedication to 'Art'], it is this bourgeois love of mine for what is human, alive and ordinary'. In *Buddenbrooks*, Mann made something that Germany's high cultural tradition could recognize as 'Art' and 'poetry' out of a loving representation of the bourgeois world that had previously been excluded from it. Only gradually did he recognize that it was necessary also to give an account of the dependence of high culture on collaboration with political authority. As the European centre of the global economy drifted towards crisis, it became generally apparent that Germany's future would be determined more by power, political and military, than by bourgeois decency and ordinariness. Mann's literary response to the crisis, the most famous of all his stories, was overwhelmingly artful but it shows the beginnings of a willingness to present German culture in a political context. 'The realm of Art is growing, and that of health and innocence is shrinking on earth' Tonio Kröger says, and in *Death in Venice* Art displaces Life everywhere. Gustav von Aschenbach, an acclaimed and mature writer, is tempted to linger too long in a cholera-ridden Venice by a homoerotic obsession with the young son of a Polish aristocratic family staying at his hotel, and succumbs to the disease. It might seem that this is another tale of Art falling in love with the Life from which it is separated and to which it pays homage. But von Aschenbach's title of nobility shows he is no Kröger: he is the offspring of a long line of servants of the Prussian state. The Art to which he has dedicated a career of self-abnegation is not the 'lively, intellectually undemanding concreteness of depiction' which entertains 'the bourgeois masses', but, we are told, philosophical, moralistic, classicizing, and highly formal. And the love to which Aschenbach surrenders is not the healthy innocence and unproblematic eros, indifferent to things of the mind, that captivates Tonio Kröger but is already aestheticized, and knowing, and explicitly not 'ordinary'. Aschenbach in his thoughts clothes it in the language of classical mythology and Nietzschean philosophy, but its true name is death – the death that in the story, in the form of a plague, is beginning to seep through the canals and squares of Venice and threatens the breakdown of all civilized order; the death that in Europe, in 1912, was marshalling its agents for the coming catastrophe, among them the Prussian soldiers and officials whose ethos Aschenbach had made his own. The irony with which Aschenbach is treated in the richly physical, but always symbolically significant, narrative medium – an art wholly different from that which is said to have made the story's hero famous – shows that Mann could express in literature a far subtler understanding of German realities than we find in the bellicose essays in which he spoke out for his country's cause after 1914.

The earth creaked before it quaked. By the early years of the 20th century prescient writers could sense that the identity of the nation, collective and individual, was threatened by the growth of global industrial mass society. Heinrich Mann recognized long before his brother that protectionist nationalism was no substitute for internationalism and could lead only to war and, in his own novels, satirized the pillars of the German state that scarcely figured in *Buddenbrooks*: academic culture in *Professor Unrat* (1905) and monarchist ideology in *His Majesty's Subject* (*Der Untertan*, 1914). Personal identity is dissolved into the interface between social role and sexual desire in the plays of Frank Wedekind (1864–1918), an unstable character, uncertain both of his national roots (he was an American citizen, and 'Frank' was short for 'Benjamin Franklin') and of his social position (after running through an inheritance he worked in Munich for Maggi Soup, and then as a cabaret artist, before he could live from his writings in a respectable marriage). *Spring's Awakening* (*Frühlings Erwachen*, 1891) was first produced in 1906 in Brahm's theatre in Berlin, by then directed by Max Reinhart, but it was not performed in full until the 1960s thanks to its scenes of flagellation, sexual intercourse, homosexual kissing, and competitive masturbation. Its fragmented manner owes much to Büchner, and its diction, combining naturalism, satirical caricature and somewhat overheated romanticism, proved very influential. Between the adult world of grotesque puppets and the unformed adolescents whose burgeoning sexuality they punish, suppress, or deny, there lies no area of mature or integral personality. Sexuality, after all, is prior to personality, and so is very close to the violence which destroys it. Lulu, the central character in Wedekind's two-part drama (1895, 1904), which gave Alban Berg the plot and title of his second opera (his first was *Wozzeck*), is more a personification of sex than a sex-driven person, and she ends as a victim of Jack the Ripper – a role which Wedekind played himself. As military confrontations such as the Moroccan crisis of 1911 showed, the power of violence that for 40 years had protected interiority was about to shake itself free. Violence figures prominently in the work of the generation of young writers who around 1910 founded journals with titles such as *Action* and *Storm*. It seems a premonition when Georg Heym (1887–1912), who died young in an accident, writes a poem about the maggots on the face of a dead soldier in a forest, but the bodies dissolving back into nature, which are the main theme of *Morgue* (1912), the first collection published by the Berlin doctor Gottfried Benn (1886–1956), are simply the material of a professional's daily work. Benn's inability to believe in personalities, let alone in relationships between them, is already apparent in his description of his affair with the Jewish poet Else Lasker-Schüler (1869–1945) as 'dark, sweet onanism'. Lasker-Schüler herself wrote, in a different vein, some of the best poetry of the period. Often gently, or eccentrically, rhymed, her poems draw on a restricted range of images – jewellery, stars, flowers, primary colours, her Jewish traditions – to explore the love of others, the world, and God. She too could sense the approach of Nietzschean apocalypse, but her poem 'World's End' (*'Weltende'*) is free of any savage or cynical heroics:

Es ist ein Weinen in der Welt,

Als ob der liebe Gott gestorben wär, […]

Du! wir wollen uns tief küssen –

Es pocht eine Sehnsucht an die Welt

An der wir sterben müssen.

[There is a weeping in the world as if the good Lord had died [...]
Come let us kiss each other deeply – there is a desire knocking at
the world and we must die of it.]

A similar sense that even amid the conflicts and absurdities of
the Second Empire a humane and compassionate life is possible
informs the most delicately humorous poetry of the period, the
'nonsense verse' of Christian Morgenstern (1871–1914). The
principal figures in his *Gallows Songs* (*Galgenlieder*, 1905, and
subsequent collections), which despite their title are rarely
macabre, are the hyper-sensitive Professor Palmström and his
friend von Korf, who to the consternation of bureaucracy has
no physical existence. In territory situated somewhat between
Edward Lear and Heath Robinson they meet the 'moonsheep'
and the 'nasobeme' (which strides around on its many
noses) and relieve stress by reading the day after tomorrow's
newspaper or inventing watches that go backwards on request.
Schoolmaster's German is parodied, dead metaphors come
back to tangible life, Palmström plays Korf's Sneezewort Sonata
on the Olfactory Organ (*Geruchsorgel*) and, decorated with
various metaphysical grace-notes, the ingenuity of the little man
cheerfully evades the constraints of a reality administered by
officials and intellectuals:

Ein finstrer Esel sprach einmal

zu seinem ehlichen Gemahl:

"Ich bin so dumm, du bist so dumm,

wir wollen sterben gehen, kumm!"

Doch wie es kommt so öfter eben:

Die beiden blieben fröhlich leben.

[A gloomy donkey once said to his wedded wife: 'I am so thick, you are so thick, let's go and die, come on'. But as tends to happen – the two stayed happily alive.]

Chapter 5
Traumas and memories
(1914–)

(i) The nemesis of 'culture' (1914–45)

The war that broke out in 1914 began the long collapse of the 19th-century attempt to organize the global economy into separate political empires. For most of the Germans who welcomed the release it brought from over a decade of increasingly ill-tempered rivalry, it was a battle against encirclement by the Triple Entente of Britain, France, and Russia. For Thomas Mann it was a battle of 'culture' against 'civilization', and of himself against his brother.

All that was truly German – he said in his two volumes of *Unpolitical Meditations* (*Betrachtungen eines Unpolitischen*, 1918) which he spent the war writing – was 'culture, soul, freedom, art, and *not* civilization, society, the right to vote, and literature'. 'Civilization' was an Anglo-French superficiality, the illusion entertained by left-wing intellectuals generally, and Heinrich Mann in particular, that the life of the mind amounted to the political agitation and social 'engagement' of journalists who thought the point of writing was to change the world. Germany, by contrast, knew that 'Art' was a deeper affair than literary chatter, and that true freedom was not a matter of parliaments and free presses but of personal, moral, duty. The Western powers, while claiming to fight for their 'freedom' against German 'militarism' were, in this view, uniting to impose their commercial mass

15. Heinrich (left) and Thomas Mann in 1927

society on Germans devoted to individual self-cultivation. Mann therefore correctly perceived the association that linked the concepts of 'Art', 'spirit', '*Bildung*', and interior Kantian 'freedom', with the hostility of the German class of officials, servants of an autocratic state, to such instruments of bourgeois self-assertion as parliamentarianism, free enterprise, and commercialized mass media. When in November 1918 the Emperor and his generals were no longer able to defend, or even to feed, the German population and handed over their responsibilities to the majority socialist party, the bureaucrats remained in office and maintained the attitudes of autocracy into the new era of parliamentary government. In Prussia, the largest state within the republic that agreed its constitution at Weimar in 1919, a socialist administration fitted seamlessly into the old structure. Oswald Spengler (1880–1936) argued in *Prussianism and Socialism* (*Preußentum und Sozialismus*, 1920) for the identity of the two systems, since both aimed to turn all workers into state officials and thereby to answer 'the decisive question, not only for Germany but for the world [...]: is commerce in future to govern the state, or the state to govern commerce?' Accepting the political revolution which, with remarkably little fuss, had put an end to German monarchy, did not imply abandoning the struggle against 'civilization'. Indeed, Spengler saw his vast 'morphological' survey of world history, *The Decline of the West* (*Der Untergang des Abendlandes*, 1918, 1922) as evidence of a pyrrhic victory of the German mind, which through him had been able to make sense of the coming displacement of traditional European culture by technological and mathematical organization.

For Germany the war did not end in 1918. Starvation, influenza, civil war, the reoccupation of territory by France to exact reparations, the economic disruption caused by the loss of population and resources and culminating in the inflation of 1923, all prolonged the conditions of wartime emergency for five years. By the time the crisis was over, the Weimar Republic consisted of a few magnates whose property interests had survived the inflation, a working population directly exposed to fluctuations in the world economy, and the administrators and beneficiaries of a welfare state 13 times larger than its equivalent in 1914. The intimations of the coming collapse of the European bourgeoisie that unsettled the pre-war world were first fulfilled in Germany. The literature of this period of revolutionary transition reflected the instability of institutions and the isolation of individuals. It was not a time for realism. It was a time for despair, abstract revolt, and utopian hopes of a new beginning. The movement of 'Expressionism' was correspondingly most active in the prophetic and emotional forms of poetry and drama. In 1920 the anthology *Twilight of Humanity* (*Menschheitsdämmerung*) brought together poems by 23 poets in the service of an indeterminate moral enthusiasm:

Ewig eint uns das Wort:

MENSCH

we are for ever united by the word 'Man'

Expressionist theatre was similarly characterized by a deliberate striving for abstractness and generality through heightened and declamatory language, but by its use of choruses, and stylization of character, it had more success than the poets in representing large-scale industrial and political conflict: the works of Reinhard Goering (1887–1936), Georg Kaiser (1878–1945), and Ernst Toller (1893–1939) are now undeservedly neglected.

Profound though the social revolution was, it did not change everything. In 1919, commenting on the atmosphere in Berlin, Albert Einstein compared Germany to 'someone with a badly upset stomach who hasn't vomited enough yet'. Once the American Dawes Plan of 1924 and a huge associated loan had stabilized the German economy, the Expressionist era was effectively over, a 'new sobriety' (*Neue Sachlichkeit*) reigned in literature, and the continuities could re-establish themselves. Weimar had seemed an appropriate place for the constituent assembly of the new republic to do its work at least partly because of the late 19th-century myth that in Goethe's Weimar a cultural nation had been born which prefigured the political nation. This mythical Weimar could now be regarded as the true and abiding Germany. Nor was the continuity simply ideological. Germany's multiple theatres survived the deposition of their princely patrons and, subsidized now by government and freed from censorship, continued to provide a forum for drama conceived as 'art' rather than simply entertainment. The Protestant clergy and, above all, the universities carried over the role of official intelligentsia that they had occupied under the monarchy into an era that, bewilderingly, lacked a monarch, and the universities almost immediately began an intellectual assault on the new republic. Martin Heidegger (1889–1976), born a Catholic at a time when Catholics were second-class Germans, converted to Lutheranism in 1919 and so gained access to the wider and better-connected world of the Protestant universities. In *Being and Time I* (*Sein und Zeit I*, 1927; Part II was never written), Heidegger strangely combined a radically depersonalized re-reading of some of the most fundamental questions in philosophy with a rather Lutheran account of individual moral salvation. His 'existentialism' thus provided both the conceptual means for rejecting contemporary society as 'inauthentic' and, with his belief that one chooses one's own history, the excuse for political activism regardless of rationality. Heidegger rapidly became an intellectual totem of the right, but Stefan George's disciples, now in professorial chairs, also had a deep influence on academic discourse in the humanities, directing it away from social and economic concerns to what became known as 'history of the mind' (*Geistesgeschichte*) and elaborating the Master's cult of the lonely, world-changing historical personality. Friedrich Gundolf (1880–1931) in Heidelberg published an epoch-making study of Goethe in 1916, and Ernst Bertram (1884–1957), professor in Bonn, published a similar study of Nietzsche in 1918, with George's swastika sign on the title page. The year 1928 saw the publication not only of a major work of literary criticism by Max Kommerell (1902–44), professor in Frankfurt and Marburg, *The Poet as Leader in German Classicism* (*Der Dichter als Führer in der deutschen Klassik*), a title which already combined the Wilhelmine vision of Germany with the National Socialist version of monarchy, but also a new and final collection of poems by George himself, *The New Empire* (*Das neue Reich*). To express a political opinion was infinitely beneath George's dignity, but it was clear from the Hölderlinian diction and military rhythms of the prophetically entitled 'To a young leader in the first world war' (*'Einem jungen Führer im ersten Weltkrieg'*) that in his view Germany's humiliation in the recent conflict was only a prelude to a greater future:

Alles wozu du gediehst rühmliches ringen hindurch

Bleibt dir untilgbar bewahrt stärkt dich für künftig getös ...

[Everything for which you grew and flourished throughout your
glorious struggle remains your indelible own, strengthens you for
future uproar ...]

Of all state employees, members of the armed forces were least likely to feel loyalty to the new régime which had signed the instruments of surrender and the Versailles Treaty. Ernst Jünger (1895–1998) fought throughout the World War with great distinction and his recollections of four years' front-line service, *Storms of Steel* (*In Stahlgewittern*, 1920), are evidence of the chilling dispassion that was necessary to survive. 'To live is to kill', he later wrote, and though the enormous success of *Storms of Steel* established him as a professional writer, he continued to speak from and to his generation's experience of mechanized mass warfare. In *The Worker* (*Der Arbeiter*, 1931), he interpreted modern economic life as an extension of the total mobilization of wartime: he rightly saw that the extinction of the bourgeoisie and proletarianization of the middle classes, already far advanced in Germany, was destined to become universal, but he wrongly assumed that only a bureaucratic and military command structure could organize the resulting industrial society. Heidegger was impressed by Jünger's analysis of the modern world, though his reaction was to turn to Hölderlin and Nietzsche as guides to Germany's future. Gottfried Benn, who had spent the war as a military doctor (and in that capacity had attended the execution of Edith Cavell), was yet more radical in his rejection of the civilian world from whose corruption he lived (he became a specialist in venereal disease). Influenced partly by Spengler, and partly by his own experiments with narcotics, he came in the 1920s to despise the superficial order modern civilization had constructed over the archaic and mythical layers of human experience: the only true order seemed to him that which he imposed on his poems, sometimes by rather too obvious force. His avowed refusal of a social role for the poet was a deliberate provocation to the socialists and communists who had figured alongside him in *Twilight of Humanity*. Like Heidegger and Jünger, however, he willingly lent an appearance of intellectual respectability to the imperious rhetoric of military leadership favoured by right-wing opponents of the republic.

Not that the left wing was any better. The Communists, bent on their own revolution, and under instructions from Moscow that their first aim must be to destroy the ruling socialist party, were as willing as the right to make use of an anti-bourgeois rhetoric which after the inflation no longer had a real object but which served to destabilize the fragile political consensus. The savage cartoons of George Grosz (1893–1959) created an image of Weimar Germany as a land of freebooting capitalism run wild, but when Grosz moved to 1930s America, where there was much more free enterprise, and much less social welfare, but where the political impetus provided by the German context was lacking,

16. Bertolt Brecht in 1927, just before the great success of *The Threepenny Opera*

his inspiration deserted him. A sense not just that politics matter, but that political institutions matter too, is lacking throughout the otherwise multifarious and often humane work of the poet and dramatist Bertolt Brecht (1898–1956).

Brecht's family, paper-makers in Augsburg, belonged to the vanishing bourgeoisie; but after he moved to Berlin in 1924 to become a professional writer-director, his study of Marxism brought him close to those who saw the future in total rule by the state, though he was never a member of the Communist Party. Instead, like Grosz, he drew grotesques, satirical, comic, sometimes even tragic, particularly of an imaginary version of the Anglo-Saxon world – whether 18th-century England, 19th-century America, or Kipling's Empire – which in the war, and in the boom years that eventually followed, seemed once again to have imposed itself on Germany as the authoritative embodiment of modernity. The jaunty discordancy of Brecht's works of the 1920s, especially his collaborations with Kurt Weill, *The Threepenny Opera* (*Die Dreigroschenoper*, 1928) and *Rise and Fall of the Town of Mahagonny* (*Aufstieg und Fall der Stadt Mahagonny*, 1928–9), derived from powerfully conflicting feelings towards this vision, or mirage, of 'capitalist' life. On the one hand, there was a mischievously amoral appetite for the opportunities of consumption and uninhibited enjoyment that it offered – a theme of Brecht's since his first play *Baal* (1918), about a poet who is as ruthlessly self-indulgent as he is totally un-self-pitying. But there was also the moral sense of official Germany, with its long tradition of being offended by irresponsible consumerism, here expressing itself in bitter satire. The driving moral force behind this economic critique, however, was not a political concern for the integrity of the state but a demand, so to speak, for hedonistic justice, for equity in the distribution of pleasure, and solidarity with those to whom pleasure is denied or for whom it is turned into pain. There was a link of substance, as well as of form, with Büchner. One of the weightiest ballads in Brecht's first collection of poems, *Domestic Breviary* (*Hauspostille*, 1927), takes up the

'Storm and Stress' theme of the infanticide mother, and the song 'Pirate Jenny' in *The Threepenny Opera* shows us a washer-up who dreams of the ship with eight sails and 50 guns that will put out its flags in her honour and then bombard the town where she suffers. But Brecht's engagement with the society of which he was a part did not extend beyond the desire to shoot it up. For all his claims that the ironical devices which made his productions both scandalous and successful were intended to set his audiences thinking about the political issues that they raised, the only institution of the Weimar Republic that Brecht's plays really concerned was the theatre. The placards descending from the flies, the direct addresses to the spectators, the parodies of grand opera, and the reduction of characters to marionettes in Wedekind's manner, all encouraged thinking, not about public affairs, but about the theatricality of the performance. It was a complete and successful break with the native German tradition of drama-as-book, but it was also an inverted aestheticism, making Art out of criticizing Art.

The same tendency to perpetuate old concepts under an appearance of criticizing the new can be found in the writings, many of them published posthumously, of Brecht's Berlin friend and admirer, Walter Benjamin (1892–1940). Benjamin attempted unsuccessfully to become a professor of German literature, and at first devoted himself to relatively unpolitical '*Geistesgeschichte*'. He later moved closer to Marxism in the quest for a more materialist theory of the relation between art and society, eventually expressed programmatically in the essay 'The work of art in the age of its technical reproducibility' ('*Das Kunstwerk im Zeitalter seiner technischen Reproduzierbarkeit*', 1936). Here he argued, rather like Brecht, that in the age of mass-media Art, being no longer able to create individual beautiful objects, had to become political. He thus overlooked the specifically German roots of the concept of 'Art', the extent to which it was part of the ideology of bureaucratic absolutism, and the consequence that to criticize society in the name of Art was to maintain the values of an oppressive era. Benjamin was for a while associated with the Institute for Social Research (Institut für Sozialforschung) in Frankfurt, founded in 1923 by the son of a millionaire corn-merchant to investigate the condition of the working classes and later incorporated into the new local university (opened in 1914). When Max Horkheimer (1895–1973) became its director in 1931, it turned to a new project: developing a critical theory of society in general. Among the brilliant talents Horkheimer briefly concentrated in Frankfurt were the Hegelian and Marxist philosopher Herbert Marcuse (1898–1979), the psychologist Erich Fromm (1900–80), and a young composer and theorist of music, Theodor Wiesengrund Adorno (1903–69), a pupil of Alban Berg. Adorno, committed to the German musical tradition and impressed by Benjamin's defence of the role of Art in modern society, was only being consistent when in 1934 he welcomed the Nazis' ban on broadcasting the degenerate American form of music known as jazz.

The Weimar Republic had few friends among its intelligentsia, but the best and most indefatigable proved, in the end, to be Thomas Mann. During the long German postlude to the war, he rather grudgingly admitted that his elder brother's politics had proved more realistic than his own, but in 1922 the murder, by right-wing extremists, of Germany's Jewish foreign minister, the respected and successful Walter Rathenau, shocked him into whole-hearted commitment to the Republican cause. Over the next ten years and with the authority, after 1929, of a Nobel prizewinner, he delivered a number of high-profile addresses in support of a system he now saw as fulfilling the promise of the German Enlightenment. At a time when hostility to a Social Democrat government, in which emancipated Jews were understandably prominent, was increasingly taking the form of anti-Semitism, he embarked on an enormous series of linked variations on biblical narratives, *Joseph and his Brothers* (*Joseph und seine Brüder*, 1933–43), that deliberately drew attention to the Jewish roots of Western history. The crisis of 1922 also enabled Mann to find a focus for the book he had been writing since 1913, *The Magic Mountain* (*Der Zauberberg*), finally published in 1924. A sanatorium in Davos provided him in this novel with a metaphor for the rarefied atmosphere of high culture in the immediately pre-war years, cosseted, morally lax, and impregnated with a sense of coming dissolution. Hans Castorp, an average 'unpolitical' German bourgeois, succumbs, in this unreal environment in which time seems to stand still, to a series of more and less intellectual temptations, from materialist science to hypochondria and sexual dalliance, from psychoanalysis to X-rays and recorded music. A half-comic, but in the end suicidally tragic, dispute on political and moral matters is maintained between Lodovico Settembrini, a representative of liberal and democratic bourgeois Enlightenment, and Leo Naphta, a Jewish Jesuit, whose arguments for amoral theocratic Terror seem – like Nietzsche, whom they echo – a nightmare condensation of the entire German official tradition, Left and Right. In an extreme and climactic moment, Hans Castorp escapes from the sanatorium into the snow but only narrowly avoids death from hypothermia. What draws him back into life is a belief in 'love and goodness' which transcends the opposition between Settembrini and Naphta. He recognizes that his German, Romantic inheritance – from Novalis to Schopenhauer, Wagner, and Nietzsche – gives him a special understanding of the background of death against which life is defined, and which, by contrast, gives life its value, but he also recognizes that 'loyalty to death and to what is past is only wickedness and dark delight and misanthropy if it determines our thinking and the way we allow ourselves to be governed'. With this insight, more exactly prophetic than any of Stefan George's oracles, Thomas Mann drew a lesson from the fall of the Second Empire which he could pass on to the Weimar Republic, and which could guide him in his own political engagement, unashamedly German, but unambiguously on the side of 'life and goodness'. Unfortunately it is an insight that Hans Castorp forgets once he is safe, and he drifts through the final stages of cultural decline into the killing fields of the World War. That too was prophetic.

Germany in the 1920s was a mature industrial state, at the forefront of technological innovation (its film industry produced more films than all its European competitors combined), with no empire, a proletarianized bourgeoisie, an active but headless official class, mass communications, and a colossal problem of identity. Its social and political postmodernity made it a natural incubator for cultural tendencies that have since spread widely as other nations have arrived in its condition. With Ernst Jünger, Carl Schmitt (1888–1985) and Leo Strauss (1899–1973) pioneered political neo-conservatism. Heidegger, one of the first to use the concept of 'deconstruction', was the fountainhead of most French philosophy in the second half of the 20th century. The physical appearance of the man-made Western world was profoundly affected by the decision of Walter Gropius (1883–1969) in 1919 to combine education in the fine arts and in crafts into a single institution in Weimar, known as the 'Bauhaus'. The idealist concept of life-transforming 'Art', united with functionalist notions of design, was here applied to mass production in industry, buildings, and furniture. In literature too there was a serious quest for ways of adapting old forms to the unprecedented circumstances of a society more deeply revolutionized in defeat than any of the victor powers. The prolific novelist Alfred Döblin (1878–1957), a Jewish doctor in the East of Berlin who eventually became a Catholic, wrote his masterpiece in *Berlin Alexanderplatz* (1929), which uses a highly fragmented manner, reminiscent of *Ulysses* (though Döblin did not know Joyce's book when he started), to evoke life in a great industrialized city. Despite its title, it is not a novel of place: Berlin in 1928 is too vast and too modern to have the cosy identity of Dublin in 1904. *Berlin Alexanderplatz* is a novel of language. The dialect of the main characters, proletarians and petty criminals, informs their semi-articulate conversations and indirectly reported thoughts, carries over into some of the various narrative voices, and is cross-cut with officialese, newspaper stories, advertisements, age-old folk songs and 1920s musical hits, parodies and quotations of the German classics, statistical reports, and the propaganda of politicians. Through this modern Babel we make out the story of the released jailbird Franz Biberkopf, big, dim, goodhearted, and shamefully abused by his friends, the breakdown of his attempt to be 'decent', and his eventual recovery (perhaps). It is a worm's-eye view of the Weimar Republic, with its socialists, communists, and anarchists fighting obscurely in the background and the National Socialists remorselessly on the rise. Marching songs and rhythms and the memory and prospect of war run as leitmotifs through the book, and the overwhelming symbol of Biberkopf's life 'under the poll-axe' is provided by a centre-piece description of the main Berlin slaughter-house, fed by converging railway lines from all over the country, a symbol more terrifyingly apposite than Döblin could know.

An intellectual's view of the destructive possibilities inherent in the directionless multiplicity of modern life was provided in 1927 by the most adventurous book of an author who had previously specialized either in monuments to self-pity or sugary (and not always well-written) stories of post-Nietzschean '*Bildung*': individuals who ripen beyond good and evil into mystical or aesthetic fulfilment. Hermann Hesse (1877–1962) did not deny his origins but he supped German life with a long spoon: born in Württemberg, he travelled in India and settled in Switzerland. *The Wolf from the Steppes* (*Der Steppenwolf*) is a transparently autobiographical account of a personal mental crisis but it is also a psychogram of the contemporary German middle classes. Harry Haller, the main narrator, personifies the disorientated '*Bildungsbürger*' in the post-war era, caught, he recognizes, between two worlds: he loves the orderliness of the bourgeoisie and lives off his investments, he is devoted to the German official culture of classical literature and music, and he also embodies the wolf-like, anti-social, Nietzschean individualism that his class has secretly fostered. However, the new, wide open, Americanized world of the 1920s, with jazz and foxtrots, gramophones and radios, offers him the possibility of dissolving the shadow side of his psyche, the wolf from the steppes, into the myriad alternative personalities latent in him and so of escaping from '*Bildungsbürgertum*' altogether. In the 'magic theatre' of the saxophonist Pablo he enjoys, as if by the aid of hallucinogenic drugs, such experiences as sleeping with all the women he has ever set eyes on, meeting Mozart (who gives him a cigarette), and playing at being a terrorist and a murderer. But evidently this is a highly ambiguous liberation. Haller, who opposed the First World War, knows that in the new age that is remaking him, 'the next war is being prepared with great zeal day by day by many thousands of people', and that it will be 'even more horrible' than the previous one, and we can see that the 'magic theatre' is one of the means by which the horror is being rehearsed. However, since Haller can no more stop war than he can stop death, he turns instead to learning to love, and to laugh at himself. Hesse is honest; he depicts both his own path to equilibrium and its cost: the withdrawal from responsibility for a monstrous, carnivorous mechanism whose workings he has understood with grim clarity.

With the crash of 1929, the time for fantasies of individual fulfilment was over. As the political tensions within the Republic reached breaking point and unemployment rose to 30%, the cultural compromise that had created the '*Bildungsbürger*' lost all plausibility. Brecht dropped his flirtation with consumerism and from 1929 to 1932 wrote a series of 'didactic plays' (*Lehrstücke*), several in cantata form, with minimal character interest, intended to encourage audiences (particularly of school-children) to think of solving problems by subordinating individual concerns, and even lives, to collective programmes. Knowing arrest was imminent, Brecht left Germany on the day after the Reichstag fire in February 1933 that gave the recently elected Nazi government the excuse to take emergency powers and introduce totalitarian rule. Those who then supported the political nationalism which was Germany's response to global economic protectionism were the immediate agents of the self-immolation of 'culture'. Heidegger, now a member of the Party, gave his inaugural address as rector of Freiburg University in May, its title, *The Self-Assertion of the German University* (*Die Selbstbehauptung der deutschen Universität*) revealing the cruel delusion of Hitler's camp-followers. For in the Third Empire there was to be no self-assertion by any institution other than the Party and its Leader, let alone by the university, which for over 300 years had been the heart of the German bureaucracy and for over 200 had given a unique character to Germany's literary culture. The final degradation of German officialdom to dutiful executants of murderous tyranny was at hand. Heidegger lent his support to the new government's rejection of globalization by campaigning for Germany's withdrawal from the League of Nations, but within a year he had resigned his office and was discarded by the regime, though he remained in the Party.

17. Martin Heidegger (indicated by the cross) at an election rally of German academics at the Alberthalle, Leipzig, on 11 November 1933

A similar fate befell Benn, seduced by the idea of 'surrendering the ego to the totality'. In a radio broadcast in April 1933, he coarsely denounced the obsolete internationalism of 'liberal intellectuals', whether Marxists who thought of nothing higher than wage-rates or 'bourgeois capitalists' who knew nothing of the world of work, and opposed to it the new totalitarian nation-state which – he claimed, combining Nietzsche and Spengler – had history and biology on its side and showed its strength by controlling the thoughts and publications of its members. So it did, and after a series of violent attacks on him in the Party press for the 'indecency' of his poems, he took cover, like Jünger, by rejoining the army – 'the aristocratic form of emigration', he said, salving the smart – and in 1938 he was officially forbidden to publish or write. Stefan George bowed out with more dignity before he died in December 1933, refusing (for unclear reasons) to serve in succession to Heinrich Mann as president of the newly purged Prussian Academy. Hauptmann stayed in Silesia, without office, but accepting honours and censorship (*The Weavers* was not to be performed) until he died after experiencing the bombing of Dresden. Otherwise, virtually all German writers and artists of significance either emigrated or withdrew from sight. German literature could be said to have been officially terminated on 10 May 1933 when the German Student Federation arranged public burnings of 'un-German works' throughout the country.

For those emigrants who survived – Benjamin committed suicide rather than fall into the hands of the Gestapo and Toller did the same out of sheer despair – exile in a non-German-speaking country where they were unknown and had little opportunity of publishing usually put the end to a literary career. Alfred Kerr (1867–1948), for example, who made and broke reputations as a theatre critic in Naturalist and Expressionist Berlin, dwindled to a refugee Jewish invalid in his London flat, though his daughter wrote a touching memoir of their life of banishment in her trilogy beginning with *When Hitler Stole Pink Rabbit*. For Brecht, however, emigration meant liberation. Until 1941 he lived mainly in Denmark and Finland, but he was already internationally known, he travelled widely, and his plays were put on in Paris, Copenhagen, New York, and Zurich. Since, however, he was writing in professional, though not personal, isolation, and no longer had his own theatre, what he wrote became gradually more reflective, less closely involved with German circumstances, and, without losing its theatricality, emotionally and psychologically more multidimensional. His poetry blossomed. He already resembled Luther and Goethe as a townsman with a love of the vernacular who had taken up with the politics of authoritarianism, and he now came to resemble them in the hide-and-seek his contradictory personality played with the public. (The theories of drama which he now elaborated were part of this game, and need not be taken seriously.) Perhaps because the public had become more difficult to define, broader both in space and time than in the Weimar forcing-house, his poetic voice achieved a new level of generality, a German voice, certainly, but addressing everyone caught up in the global conflict:

Was sind das für Zeiten, wo

Ein Gespräch über Bäume fast ein Verbrechen ist

Weil es ein Schweigen über so viele Untaten einschließt! […]

Ihr, die ihr auftauchen werdet aus der Flut

In der wir untergegangen sind

Gedenkt

Wenn ihr von unseren Schwächen sprecht

Auch der finsteren Zeit

Der ihr entronnen seid. ('An die Nachgeborenen')

[What sort of times are these when a conversation about trees is
almost a crime because it includes silence about so many misdeeds
[...] You who will emerge from the tide in which we have sunk,
remember too, when you speak of our weaknesses, the dark time
from which you have escaped.]

('To later generations', 1939)

From 1938 Brecht was writing what were effectively morality
plays for a world audience, in which the deeper themes of his early
work returned: his passionate sense that pleasure and goodness
are what human beings are made for and that justice requires
that pleasure should be universal and goodness rewarded; his
bitter countervailing belief that injustice is general, that it is
often necessary for the survival even of the good, and that it may
be remediable only by unjust means; and a Marxism which is
not a source of answers to these dilemmas, but a background
conviction that answers are possible and so should be looked for.
The Good Woman of Szechuan (*Der gute Mensch von Sezuan*,
1938–9, first performed 1943) was still just about interpretable
as a demonstration that in capitalist society moral goodness was
necessarily symbiotic with economic exploitation, if the anguished
love of the 'good woman' herself was overlooked, but *The Life
of Galileo* (*Leben des Galilei*, 1938–9, first performed 1943) was
Brecht's most personal play, and despite extensively adapting
it after 1945, he was unable to fit it into a Marxist scheme. The
pleasure-loving genius with a huge appetite for life who fails the
political test and recants when threatened by the Inquisition, but
who argues that he serves progress better by devious compliance
than by pointless heroism, clearly embodies some of Brecht's
own feelings about the priority he was giving – and had always
given – to his literary work over the political struggle. His one
genuinely tragic play, *Mother Courage and her Children* (*Mutter
Courage und ihre Kinder*, 1939, first performed 1941), though
written before war had broken out, was the nearest he came in a
major drama to commentary on the great events of his age. Set in
early 17th-century Germany, in a state of war without beginning

or end, it dramatizes 'the dark time' in which Brecht's generation had, somehow or other, to live. Mother Courage, who has little more than her name in common with Grimmelshausen's character (and even that has lost most of its sexual connotations), drags her sutler's wagon after the marauding armies on which she depends for a livelihood. Her calculating, unscrupulous, shopkeeper's realism – like Galileo's cunning – makes sense for as long as it serves the purpose of keeping her family alive and together. But one by one she loses her children to different forms of the goodness she has warned them against. Alone at the end, she has survived – but what for? It was Brecht's own question to himself.

In 1941 Brecht left Finland for Russia and, without stopping to inspect the workings of socialism, took the trans-Siberian route to the Pacific Ocean and California. There he met W. H. Auden (who thought him the most immoral man he had ever known) and found a colony of German émigrés, such as Erich Maria Remarque (1898–1970), author of the gripping pot-boiler *All Quiet on the Western Front* (*Im Westen nichts Neues*, 1929), many of them attracted, like him, by the prospect of work in Hollywood. There too Brecht wrote his happiest – and last significant – play, *The Caucasian Chalk Circle* (*Der kaukasische Kreidekreis*, 1944–5, first performed 1948, in English). In it the pure, self-sacrificing love of another 'good woman' and the self-preserving immoralism of an unjust judge, embodied in characters as fully drawn as Mother Courage or Galileo, are united in a moment 'almost of justice', while Marxism is relegated to sedately utopian, socialist-realist framework scenes which pretend to underwrite the hope expressed in the principal action. Not all of Brecht's fellow exiles were as easily reconciled to life in the USA, however. Horkheimer and Adorno managed to re-establish the Institute of Social Research in California and tried there to use the inherited concepts of German philosophy to explain the barbarism engulfing Europe. But their joint study, *Dialectic of Enlightenment* (*Dialektik der Aufklärung*, 1944), suffers, like the Marxist tradition itself, and like Brecht's feeble attempts at direct representation of the Nazi regime, from an inadequate theory of politics (treated simply as a cloak for economic interests) and from a limited understanding of the special character of the German society from which they came. It was boorish and inept to equate the capitalism of America, which was paying in blood to save their lives and their work, with genocidal Fascism (as Brecht also did in his lesser plays). Their assault on the American entertainment industry was not just the snobbery of expatriates from the homeland of Art: Adorno and Horkheimer explicitly defended, against the mass market and mass politics that had swept them away, 19th-century Germany's 'princes and principalities', the 'protectors' of the institutions – 'the universities, the theatres, the orchestras and the museums' – which had maintained the idea of a freedom available through Art and transcending the (supposedly) false freedoms of economic and political life. In thus preparing to hand on to a later generation, as the key to modern existence, the concepts and slogans of the defunct German conflict between bourgeoisie and bureaucracy, Adorno and Horkheimer committed themselves to much the same half-truths as a writer for whom they had no time at all, Hermann Hesse.

In 1943 Hesse issued from his Swiss retreat his own reaction to the contemporary crisis, *The Glass-Bead Game* (*Das Glasperlenspiel*), a novel of personal '*Bildung*' set in the distant future and in the imaginary European province of Castalia. As the allusion to the Muses' sacred spring suggests, Castalia is devoted to Art, but an Art which has absorbed all previous forms of artistic and intellectual expression into a single supreme activity, the Glass-Bead Game. A secular monastic order is dedicated to the cultivation of the Game, and the novel tells of the development of its greatest master, Josef Knecht, to the point where he recognizes the need to relate this religion of Art to the world beyond it. Castalia is threatened by war, economic pressures, and political hostility, as in the 'warlike age' of the mid-20th century, in which the Game originated. Knecht's end, however, and that of the novel, is obscure: has he indeed secured the survival of the Castalia that preserves his memory? Or has he, as his Castalian successors would clearly like to believe, betrayed Art to Life and been punished accordingly? The Castalian world of the Spirit (*Geist*) seems hermetically detached from the historical world of society, and even if Spirit is in reality dependent on Society, it seems not to acknowledge, or even to know, that it is. Hesse's anxiety about the ability of Art and the Spirit to survive into the post-war era is expressed with more modesty, and greater political astuteness, than we find in *Dialectic of Enlightenment*, but he is no more able than Adorno and Horkheimer to represent those concepts as peculiar to a particular time and place and tradition.

That was to be the task of another German resident of California, Thomas Mann, who had arrived in America in 1939, and from 1943, following daily the news of Germany's military collapse, worked intensively on his greatest novel, completed and published in 1947, *Doctor Faustus. The life of the German composer Adrian Leverkühn, narrated by a friend* (*Doktor Faustus. Das Leben des deutschen Tonsetzers Adrian Leverkühn erzählt von einem Freunde*). Mann consulted Adorno about his manuscript, particularly its musical sections, and sent Hesse a copy of the published work with the inscription, 'the glass-bead game with black beads', but his book went to the heart of the issue that their books evaded. *Doctor Faustus* is a reckoning with the German past at many levels. It gives a fictionalized account of the social and intellectual world of the Second Empire and the Weimar Republic, particularly Munich (complete with proto-fascist poets). In taking the life of Nietzsche as its model for the life-story of Adrian Leverkühn, and his apparent purchase of world-changing artistic achievement at the cost of syphilitic dementia, it asserts the typicality of a figure whose thinking was all-pervasive in 20th-century Germany and who contributed in his own way to what passed for Nazi ideology. It is shot through with allusions to earlier phases of destructive irrationalism in German literature and history, and above all it appropriates the central myth of modern German literature to suggest that the story of Leverkühn parallels the story of modern Germany, for both are the story of a Faustian pact with the devil. Links with contemporary reality punctuate the narrative, which is in the hands of Leverkühn's friend, Serenus Zeitblom, a retired schoolteacher, who starts his work, like Mann, in 1943 and ends in the chaos of total defeat in 1945. The ultimate refinement in this supremely complex work, however, is that, for all the apparent concentration on the artist figure Leverkühn and his assimilation to the figure of Faust, the true representative of Germany in it is Zeitblom. Zeitblom is a state official, steeped in the classics and German literature, who shares Thomas Mann's 'unpolitical' attitude to the First World War, but not his post-war conversion; he does not emigrate, he has two Nazi sons, and he dissents from Hitler's policies only quietly, on aesthetic grounds, and as they start to fail. Germany's fate is here represented not by Faust, Art, and the life lived *in extremis*, but by the man who believes in these ideas, who needs them to give colour and significance to his life, and who structures his narrative in accordance with them. The moral climax of the book, the point when it represents directly the sadistic monstrosity of the Third Reich, is Zeitblom's chapter-long account of the agonizing death from meningitis of Leverkühn's five-year-old nephew, supposedly fetched by the devil. For a dozen pages this narrator tortures a child to death to justify his own desire to live out a myth. His fellows did as much across German-occupied Europe. In Zeitblom (the name means 'flower of the age'), Thomas Mann created an image of the German class that saw itself as defined by 'culture' and that accepted Hitler as its monarch, its metaphysical destiny, and its nemesis.

(ii) Learning to mourn (1945–)

In 1967 the psychologists Alexander and Margarete Mitscherlich (1908–82 and 1917–) published *The Inability to Mourn* (*Die Unfähigkeit zu trauern*), an analysis of Germany's collective reaction to the trauma of 1945, the 'zero hour' in German history when the past was lost, the present was a ruin, and the future was a blank. Their conclusion was that there had been no reaction: Germany had frozen emotionally, had deliberately forgotten both its huge affective investment in the Third Reich and the terrible human price paid by itself and others to rid it of that delusion, had shrugged off its old identity and identified instead with the victors (whether America in the West or Russia in the East), and had thrown itself into the mindless labour of reconstruction, which created the Western 'economic miracle' and made East Germany the most successful economy in the Soviet bloc. This analysis, and in particular its conclusion that Nazi thinking was still as omnipresent in (West) German society as the old Nazis themselves, had a powerful influence on the revolutionary generation of 1968 and reinforced the accepted wisdom that 'coming to terms with the past' (*Vergangenheitsbewältigung*) was the major task of contemporary literature. But there was a good deal more to mourn than unacknowledged Nazism, repressed memories of Nazi crimes, the horrors of civilian bombardment, the misery of military defeat, or the uncomfortable fact that in the four years before the foundation of the two post-war German states in 1949 the prevailing mood was not joy and relief but sullen resentment both of the Allies and of the German emigrants. There was the further complication that the past calling out to be reassessed did not begin in 1933, it was potentially as old as Germany itself, while the present, for all the talk of reconstruction, had no historical precedents. It might resemble the aftermath of the Thirty Years War, though without the princes, but more importantly it was without a bourgeoisie: both German states were workers' states – one was just wealthier than the other. But because in the Eastern German state the absolutist rule of officials survived under the name of 'socialism', it created an image of its Western rival on the model of officialdom's old enemy and characterized the Federal Republic as 'bourgeois' Germany. With the building of the Wall in 1961, this double illusion was set in concrete and barbed wire and exercised an increasingly malign influence on German intellectual life on both sides of the barrier. For the greatest obstacle to clear-sighted assessment of the present and the past was a factor which the Mitscherlichs did not mention: that neither of the world powers which had divided Germany between them wished to encourage it. Rather, they wanted their front-line German states, between which the Iron Curtain ran, to understand themselves as showcases for their respective blocs in the bipolar global system. 'Denazification' procedures were stopped in the West, and held to be unnecessary in the East. Only after 1990 were German writers released from this imposed and misleading confrontation, and as they became free to understand Germany's position in a global market and a global culture in which national identities had long been dissolving, they also became free to address their own history.

After 1945, many emigrants stayed where they were or avoided settling in Germany. By this time they were anyway largely exhausted. Thomas Mann, who returned to Switzerland, and Hesse, who continued to live there, were honoured – Hesse with the Nobel Prize in 1946 – but unproductive. The Communists returned to the Russian zone, but apart from Brecht they had little international standing. Adorno came back in 1949 to a professorship in Frankfurt, where the Institute for Social Research was reopened in 1951. In the West the task of reacting in literature to the traumatic past was in the hands of a new generation of ex-servicemen and ex-prisoners of war, many of whom arranged to meet annually to discuss their work and became known as 'Group 47' (*Gruppe 47*). For this new generation, the problem of inheritance was particularly evident in poetry. Adorno's famous dictum of 1949 that 'to write poetry after Auschwitz is barbaric' reflected partly the special role of lyrical poetry in Germany as the literary medium for the exploration of individual ethical experience. That this role was over was emphatically stated in the last phase of the work of Gottfried Benn, which became known to the public in the early 1950s. Despite the Nazi prohibition, he had continued to write in secret, especially what he called 'static poems', regular in form and rich in imagery of autumn and extinction. A collection privately circulated in 1943 contained one of his greatest poems, 'Farewell' (*'Abschied'*), a tormented admission that in 1933 he had betrayed 'my word, my light from heaven', and that it was impossible to come to terms with such a past: *'Wem das geschah, der muß sich wohl vergessen'* ('Anyone to whom that happened will have to forget himself'). After this personal outcry, his public stance of unyielding nihilism, in the post-war years, was entirely consistent:

es gibt nur zwei Dinge: die Leere

und das gezeichnete Ich

[there are only two things: emptiness and the constructed self]

('*Nur zwei Dinge*', 1953)

If the self has become pure construction, not made out of interactions with its past experiences or with a given world, there is no place for poetry as it had been practised in Germany from Goethe to Lasker-Schüler. The poet who showed Adorno that it was still possible to write poetry in the knowledge of Auschwitz had certainly understood this lesson. There is no role for a self, or for any controlling construction, in the work of Paul Celan (1920–70), a German Jew from Romania, both of whose parents were killed in a death-camp, and who chose to live in Paris, where he committed suicide.

Celan is best known for the finest single lament for the Jewish genocide, 'Death Fugue' (*'Todesfuge'*), an erratic block in the otherwise over-lush collection *Poppies and Memory* (*Mohn und Gedächtnis*, 1952), but he seems to have felt that even this impersonal, repetitive musical structure, with its motifs of 'black milk', 'ashen hair', the name of Jewish beauty, '*Sulamit*', and the terrifying climactic phrase 'death is a master from Germany' (*'der Tod ist ein Meister aus Deutschland'*), imposed too much of a subjective order on a strictly unthinkable event.

18. **Paul Celan in 1967**

In his later collections (e.g. *Speechgrid* [*Sprachgitter*], 1959; *Breathturn* [*Atemwende*], 1967), he thought of the poem as a 'meridian', an imaginary line both linking disparate words and names and events and, by its arbitrariness, holding them apart, so re-enacting the meaninglessly violent juxtapositions and discontinuities of 20th-century history. Although many of the elements, including the vocabulary, are hermetically personal, the call for interpretation that these Webern-like miniatures embody makes them strangely public statements in which the anguish of the bereaved survivor is largely uncontaminated by Germany's growing ideological division.

> [...] *Stimmen* im Innern der Arche:
>
> Es sind
>
> nur die Münder
>
> geborgen. Ihr
>
> Sinkenden, hört
>
> auch uns. [...]
>
> [*Voices* inside the Ark: Only our mouths are rescued. You who are sinking, hear us too]

At the same time as Benn was marking the end of poetry as the coherent utterance of a solitary private voice, Brecht was providing it with a new role as the public voice of personal political engagement. He proved by far the strongest influence on the poetry of both the Federal and the Democratic Republics, but the influence was as ambiguous as the engagement. Brecht had returned to Europe in 1947 and, prevented by the Americans from entering the Western zone, settled instead in the East, where he was given a theatre and a privileged position as the jewel in the new republic's cultural crown. While he did not publicly oppose the military suppression of the workers' revolt in 1953, he wrote a series of epigrammatic poems sardonically distancing himself from the action (perhaps the government should elect itself a new people?) and asserting, presumably as a justification of his position as court poet, the social value of literary pleasure. The example both of this last, laconic manner and of his earlier more discursive poetry enabled later poets to address public issues with directness and, often, lightness of touch. But his accommodation with the Communist régime and his failure to unmask either its false claim to cultural continuity with the German 'classical heritage' or the reality of its institutional continuity with the bureaucracy of the Third and Second Empires set a bad precedent. Even the most gifted West German poet of the next generation, Hans Magnus Enzensberger (born 1929), succumbed to the assumption that the complacencies and contradictions of life in the Federal Republic lit up by his satirical fireworks were somehow a consequence of the division of the world between Right and Left. It seemed to him (as it did to all of us) that to be modern was to be subject to the threat of thermonuclear Mutual Assured Destruction by these two opposing systems. When, therefore, he wrote a counter-poem to Brecht's 'To later generations', he began it with an equation of the Cold War and the Second War which became obsolete in 1989:

wer soll da noch auftauchen aus der flut,

wenn wir darin untergehen?

[who else is supposed to emerge from the tide if we sink in it?]

('Extension' ['*Weiterung*'])

By contrast, Celan's revision of Brecht's poem gets much closer to the heart of Germany's difficulty with its past-haunted present. Poetry, Celan knew, needed a purification of language and memory, not the prescription of acceptable topics:

[…] Was sind das für Zeiten,

wo ein Gespräch

beinah ein Verbrechen ist,

weil es soviel Gesagtes

mit einschließt?

[What sort of times are these when any conversation is almost a crime because it includes so much that has been said?]

('A Leaf' ['*Ein Blatt*'], 1971)

In drama, Brecht, of course, was everywhere. He wrote nothing of importance after his return to Germany, but in his decade with the Berliner Ensemble he created a model of modernist, politically didactic theatre which, while at first having little effect on the resolutely Second Empire traditions of production in the East, gained great authority in the West, especially after 1968, and made it possible to conceal a lack of direct engagement with the literary heritage beneath an appearance of critical detachment. The institutional continuity, however, was virtually unbroken: as in 1918, Germany's theatres survived the revolution and not for 20 years did major new writing talent emerge. Even then the function assigned to the theatre by a new generation of producers and writers was what it had always been, except in the brief bourgeois period before 1914 – to be a state institution in which the intellectual elite could through Art perfect the morals of the citizens (or subjects). The plays of Rolf Hochhuth (born 1931) do not deny their Schillerian ancestry. His denunciation of Pope Pius XII for complicity in the murder of Europe's Jews (*The Representative* [*Der Stellvertreter*], 1963) was written in five acts and a form of blank verse, and concentrated on issues of personal moral responsibility. Hochhuth's determination to find highly placed individuals to blame for great crimes – Churchill in *Soldiers* (*Soldaten*, 1967); Hans Filbinger, the prime minister of Baden-Württemberg, in *Lawyers* (*Juristen*, 1979) – was on occasion highly effective (Filbinger was forced to resign). But it did not help a broader understanding of the historical and cultural context that made the crimes possible. Moral improvement might not seem to be the purpose of the explosively entertaining and hugely successful first play of Peter Weiss (1916–82), a Jewish emigrant and Communist who had lived in Sweden since 1939. *The Persecution and Murder of Jean Paul Marat Represented by the Theatre Company of the Hospital of Charenton under the Direction of M. de Sade*, usually known as *Marat/Sade* (1964), plays to the gallery with sex, violence, and madness, slithering between illusion and reality, with songs and self-conscious effects in the manner of the early Brecht, and with an early Brechtian theme: the conflict between the isolated hedonist, Sade, and Marat, the spokesman of impersonal and collective revolutionary action. But Weiss himself saw it as a Marxist play, and in his next, much grimmer, work, *The Investigation (Die Ermittlung,* 1965), a documentary drama drawing on the transcripts of the recent trial in Frankfurt of some of the staff in Auschwitz, he selected his material in accordance with the thesis of Brecht's Third Reich plays: that Hitler could be explained by the logic of big business. Weiss's ideas were formed in the 1930s and contributed minimally to German self-understanding. The three volumes of his last work, the novel *Aesthetics of Resistance (Ästhetik des Widerstands,* 1975–81), reiterated the fallacy that had done so much damage in the inter-war years: that '*Bildung*' was a supra-historical value with no particular basis in the German class structure. In the GDR, by contrast, Heiner Müller (1929–95), as director of the Berliner Ensemble, combined his own passionate demand for humanistic socialism, which he felt states always betray, with Brechtian devices taken to a postmodernist extreme, to create extraordinarily powerful works which frequently proved too much for the GDR authorities and had little in common with the armchair leftism prevalent in the Federal Republic. In a loose cycle which opened with *Germania Death in Berlin (Germania Tod in Berlin,* 1977) and closed with its intertextual counterpart *Germania 3 Ghosts at The Dead Man (Germania 3 Gespenster am Toten Mann,* 1996), a lament for the GDR, Müller puts bodies, language, and history through the mincing machine; cannibalism, mutilation, and sexual perversion abound; theatrical conventions are strained to the limit and beyond; and the contributions of Prussian militarism, Nazism, and Stalinism to the formation of the modern German states are brutally demonstrated. These plays have the uninhibited wildness of true mourning. However, since their underlying assumption is that the real victim of the German past has been socialism, they are mourners at the wrong funeral.

As for narrative prose, the sharpest insights tend to be found at the beginning of the period of German division, before the confrontation of the two republics had been consolidated. Much of the best writing of Heinrich Böll (1917–85) is in the disillusioned and understated short stories he wrote in the immediate post-war years: stories of military chaos and defeat, of shattered cities and lives, of the black market, hunger, and cigarettes. *Traveller, if you come to Spa ... (Wanderer, kommst du nach Spa ... , 1950)* is the interior monologue of a fatally wounded ex-sixth-former carried to an emergency operating theatre in the school he left only months before. He recognizes the room from a fragment of Simonides' epigram on Thermopylae which he had himself written on the blackboard, and most of the brief narrative is taken up with enumeration of the cultural objects that still litter the corridors – the bust of Caesar, the portraits of Frederick the Great and Nietzsche, the illustrations of Nordic racial types. The bloodstained downfall of '*Bildung*' has been given us in cruel miniature. Böll's most ambitious investigation of the Nazi infection in the German body politic was the novel *Billiards at 9.30 (Billard um halbzehn*, 1959), which spans the period from the end of the 19th century to 1958. Three generations of an architect family have been involved with a Benedictine monastery: the grandfather built it; the father blew it up in the Second World War, nominally for military reasons, but in fact because he knew it to be corrupted by Nazism; the son is rebuilding it, unaware who was responsible for its destruction.

Round this theme is woven a picture of a society in which former criminals, their victims, and their opponents mingle on equal or unequal, but usually unjust, terms. During the Adenauer years, Böll, also a Catholic Rhinelander, seems to have seen himself as the moral conscience of a Church compromised by its wartime record and by its association with wealth and power in the new and predominantly Catholic Germany. But in his later work the sense of a historically defined Germany measured by an external standard of justice faded, the targets of his critiques became more secular, and his position became more simply that of socialist opposition to the Christian Democrat Party (e.g. *The Lost Honour of Katharina Blum* [*Die verlorene Ehre der Katharina Blum*], 1974). Böll remained interested in modernist techniques such as multiple, undefined, or unreliable narrative viewpoints, but the clunking symbolism and schematic morality already apparent in *Billiards at 9.30* became more pronounced and his original fierce identification with a unique moment in the national life was lost.

Günter Grass (born 1927) followed a course rather like Böll's, though Böll got his Nobel Prize in 1972, while Grass, more of an *enfant terrible*, had to wait until 1999. Grass is a poet, dramatist, graphic artist, and prolific novelist, but he will be remembered above all for one book. *The Tin Drum* (*Die Blechtrommel*, 1959) is the life story of Oskar Matzerath, who begins, like Grass, on the interface between the German and Polish communities in Danzig, who decides at the age of three to stop growing, who drifts, lecherous and seemingly invulnerable, though armed only with his tin drum and a voice that can break glass when he sings, through the absurdist horrors of the Third Reich, and who is finally incarcerated in a lunatic asylum in the Federal Republic where he composes his memoirs. The novel stands out from everything else written, by Grass or others, about the Nazi period for the amoral exuberance of its narration. Oskar is, at most, passingly puzzled by the eagerness of these adults to destroy each other and the nice things he enjoys. The amorality is

19. *The Tin Drum*: Günter Grass (left), with David Bennent (as Oskar Matzerath, with drum) and Volker Schlöndorff (director), during the filming in Danzig (Gdansk), 1979

essential, for it reflects that of the acts and actors that are being described. So too is the exuberance, for against all the evil and death, from which the book refuses to avert its gaze, it asserts the value of life and pleasure – the untiring verbal inventiveness, some of it encouraged by Döblin's example, is a sustained act of resistance. But the crucial device that makes *The Tin Drum* into an exceptionally powerful analysis of how the German catastrophe happened is its parodistic relation to the German literary tradition – specifically to the tradition since the last comparable catastrophe, the Thirty Years War. Grass goes back to the early sections of Grimmelshausen's *Simplicissimus* to find a narrative standpoint from which he can encompass a political development that ends in Nazism and a literary development that ends in Oskar Matzerath. Oskar learns to read from Goethe's novel of personal maturing, *Wilhelm Meister*, regarded since the Second Empire as the fountainhead of '*Bildung*', and from a life of Rasputin. That

Goethe and Rasputin could also, grotesquely, go hand in hand in German 20th-century history is shown by a novel in which every convention of '*Bildung*' is overturned, starting with the idea of personal growth, and the course of events seems to be determined not by Nature or Spirit but by a homicidal maniac. In Grass's later works – even the next two books in what the English scholar John Reddick has called his 'Danzig trilogy' – the inventiveness became arch or stilted and the themes lost urgency as they became politically correct (e.g. *The Flounder* [*Der Butt*], 1977). The Wall made not only the GDR but the Federal Republic too a more introverted place and, responding to the need to defend public life from the left-wing Fascism of the Baader-Meinhof gang, and perhaps inspired by the example of Thomas Mann, Grass became a reliable and important campaigner for the Social Democrat Party as he became a less penetrating analyst of his world.

Because much of the writing of Arno Schmidt (1914–79) was done in the 1950s, and from 1958 he led the life of a (married and atheist) hermit in rural lower Saxony, he was insulated from these local difficulties and maintained, partly thanks to his enormous erudition, a broader view of German nationhood. *The Heart of Stone* (*Das steinerne Herz*, 1956) balanced an unflattering picture of both the modern zones with a sub-plot dependent on the earlier trauma from which the contemporary division of Germany derived: the absorption of the independent principalities, in this case the Kingdom of Hanover, into Bismarck's Empire. In *The Republic of Scholars* (*Die Gelehrtenrepublik*, 1957), Schmidt wrote a science-fiction parable of the Cold War, that other and larger-scale determinant of German identities, set in a post-World War Three era, when German is a dead language. Schmidt's eccentricities of style, spelling, and punctuation were part of his deliberate detachment from his contemporaries and should not be dismissed simply as pastiche of Joyce – though his *magnum opus*, *Bottom's Dream* (*Zettel's Traum*, 1970), 1,300 multi-columned A3 pages weighing over a stone, owed much to *Finnegan's Wake*.

Uwe Johnson (1934–84) chose a different way to preserve his independence and his ability to write, moving from East to West Germany in 1959, spending much of the 1960s abroad, and settling in England in 1974. He developed a narrative method without a privileged narrator of any kind, piecing together fragments of discourse in a montage which eventually made extensive use of newspaper material: there is no single truth about the lives of his characters or about their relation to the major public events which intimately affect them. *Speculations about Jakob* (*Mutmaßungen über Jakob*, 1959) treats the murky circumstances surrounding the death of a man who is a 'stranger in the West, but no longer at home in the East' at the time of the Hungarian uprising and the Suez crisis, while *The Third Book about Achim* (*Das dritte Buch über Achim*, 1961) asks whether a personality is continuous across the divide between the Nazi years and the GDR and finds no answer. The possibility of socialism with a human face, already an issue in *Speculations about Jakob*, is a central theme in the four volumes of *Anniversaries* (*Jahrestage*, 1971–83), which take up some of the same characters and follow every day of their lives throughout the year 1967–8, cross-cutting the German past, the American present, and the crushing of the Prague Spring. In comparison with these powerful books, the experiments in narrative indeterminacy of Christa Wolf (born 1929), who stayed in the GDR, joining the party hierarchy and literary bureaucracy, seem relatively colourless. *The Quest for Christa T.* (*Nachdenken über Christa T*, 1968) shows little awareness of the social constituents of personality, despite spanning the same period as *The Third Book about Achim*. Her autobiographical *Patterns of Childhood* (*Kindheitsmuster*, 1976), however, impressively presents both the illusions of a Nazi childhood and the traumatic effect of the transition to the later standpoint from which she tries to write.

Since 1945 the challenge facing Germans writing about Germans has been to transform trauma into memory and to understand the present by mourning the past, to show what it is to be German by telling stories broad and deep enough to contain the indescribable. After 1961 that challenge became even more difficult, and only those whose narrative could rise to include the global power relationships which were imposing on Germany an economic, social, and cultural schizophrenia had any chance of success. Only a resolutely international or historical perspective could resist the hypnotic attraction of the great lie on which German division was based: that the Democratic Republic was a nation freely working to realize socialism, when it was actually, as the Wall proclaimed, an old-fashioned bureaucratic dictatorship maintained by the military force of a foreign power. Such a perspective was easier to attain in philosophy than in literature. Heidegger and Jünger in their later, and unrepentant, work perhaps achieved it, if for quite the wrong reasons. Adorno paid a cruel penalty for his continued adherence to '*Bildung*' when he was pilloried by students as a reactionary and, probably as a result, died of a heart attack in 1969; but the tradition of the 'Frankfurt School' was carried on and decisively broadened by his pupil Jürgen Habermas (born 1929). Habermas sought a synthesis of German philosophy with the American and British traditions (rejected by Adorno) in a theory of evolving democratic argument: in democracies Enlightenment was embodied in institutions (*The Theory of Communicative Action* [*Theorie des kommunikativen Handelns*], 1981). He thereby both related the constitutional order of the Federal Republic to that of other Western nations and marked it off critically from the German past. His fear that, none the less, the government of Helmut Kohl was encouraging a nationalist form of West German patriotism which would efface the difference between the Federal Republic and earlier German states was expressed in 1986–7 in his criticisms of revisionist historians of the Jewish genocide (the 'battle of the historians', or '*Historikerstreit*'). Arguably, however, Kohl was consciously concerned only that Germany should also mourn its 11 million casualties of the Second World War: a true assessment of the Third Reich was possible only if its full cost was recognized.

That goal came significantly nearer in 1989 with Russia's withdrawal of military cover from Eastern Europe and the collapse of its puppet regimes. In East Germany the last survival from the era of bureaucratic absolutism came to an inglorious end, and with it 30 years of false consciousness for the whole nation. Those, like Christa Wolf, who had already once rebuilt their lives on those hollow foundations could not be expected to reconstruct themselves after a second trauma. But for established Western writers and younger writers from the East a new degree of honesty became possible. After an angry critique of Kohl's handling of reunification that was more a political intervention than a novel (*Too far afield* [*Ein weites Feld*], 1996), Grass returned to something like his old form with *Crabwalk* (*Im Krebsgang*, 2002), centred on the flight of East Prussians from the advancing Russian armies in 1945 and the torpedoing of a refugee ship with the loss of 9,000 lives. His admission of service in the Waffen-SS in his autobiography of 2006 also showed that his portrait of Oskar Matzerath was closer to reality than anyone had been prepared to allow when *The Tin Drum* was first published. In 2005 the prizewinning poet Durs Grünbein (born 1962) attempted to address the most notorious of all Allied war crimes, the fire-bombing of Dresden, from the point of view of a native of the city, taking into account Dresden's political and cultural history, its associations with the Nazis and its dismal reconstruction in the GDR: incongruities of tone were essential to the poem but brought it a mixed reception (*Porcelain. Poem on the death of my city* [*Porzellan. Poem vom Untergang meiner Stadt*]). Germany's inability to mourn the terrible bombing campaign against its cities had been the subject of a controversial study by W. G. ('Max') Sebald (1944–2001), *On the Natural History of Destruction* (literally: *Literature and the War in the Air* [*Luftkrieg und Literatur*], 1999), itself a sign that the taboo was being broken. Sebald's novels, the most striking event in German literature of the 1990s, are both single-minded and endlessly varied in their concentration on the process of remembering past violence, the process by which, as we are told in *The Emigrants* (*Die Ausgewanderten*, 1992), a dead body, snowed up on the mountainside, will eventually, after many years, emerge at the foot of a glacier. Like Uwe Johnson, Sebald, long a professor at the University of East Anglia, had to settle outside Germany in order to give his memory the freedom and scope necessary for his literary project. The lives and deaths that his stories retrieve from the ice ramify round the world. Though the German catastrophe is usually their overt or covert point of reference, they involve highly detailed presentations of many seemingly unrelated topics and locales: Istanbul and North America, the architecture of railway stations, the history of the silk industry, and the works of Sir Thomas Browne. Germany appears to be quite tangential to *The Rings of Saturn. An English Pilgrimage* (*Die Ringe des Saturn. Eine englische Wallfahrt*, 1995), which is concerned (as the title indicates) with the patterns made by the debris left over from another world-historical implosion, that of the British Empire. By his deliberate ambiguity of genre – are we reading fiction, autobiography, history, or documentary?; are the blurred photographs scattered through the narrative authentic or staged, relevant or irrelevant? – Sebald replicates both the layers of forgetting that have to be excavated to get at the past and the variety, always eluding unity, in what we are trying to recover. The books have a unity, however, and it lies in something wholly German: their cultivation of exquisitely calm, statuesque, and elaborate sentences which, apart from little, scarcely noticeable, 20th-century spoilers, could have been written by Goethe. It is these which tell us that this view of our present condition, global though it is in its reach, is achieved from a historically and culturally particular standpoint – a tragic standpoint because it is German and because in no other language would it have been necessary or possible to write Sebald's greatest single sentence, a ten-page account of the concentration camp in Theresienstadt, in his last novel, *Austerlitz* (2001). Sebald's work is a clear sign that since the turning point (*Wende*) of 1989–90, German literature has resumed its original post-war search for a national historical identity, a search that is important to all of us, not just because every nation has similarly to find its place in an ever more integrated world system, but because the German example makes it peculiarly clear that what matters in the end is not identity, national or personal, but the pursuit of justice.

Further reading

The following list details some of the best writing in English on the topics touched on here and also serves as an acknowledgement of some of this book's main sources.

German history

Hagen Schulze, *Germany: A New History*, tr. Deborah Lucas Schneider (Harvard University Press, 1998). Excellent concise introduction with useful material on cultural history.

Eda Sagarra, *A Social History of Germany 1648–1914* (Methuen, 1977). Comprehensive synthesis that keeps the implications for literature always in view.

W. H. Bruford, *Germany in the Eighteenth Century: The Social Background of the Literary Revival* (Cambridge University Press, 1965). Foundational study, still unsurpassed.

Histories of German literature

The Cambridge History of German Literature, ed. Helen Watanabe-O'Kelly (Cambridge University Press, 1997, 2000). Full, reliable, up-to-date, traditional literary history with extensive bibliographies.

A New History of German Literature, ed. David E. Wellbery, and others (Harvard University Press, 2006). 188 individual essays, interrelated but avoiding a single narrative.

Philosophy and German Literature,1700–1990, ed. Nicholas Saul
(Cambridge University Press, 2002). Authoritative treatment of
this crucial aspect.

The Oxford Companion to German Literature, ed. Henry Garland and
Mary Garland, 3rd edn (Oxford University Press, 1997). Dictionary
format, with over 6,000 entries.

Collections of essays

Erich Heller, *The Disinherited Mind* (Bowes & Bowes, 1952, and
numerous subsequent editions). Studies of Goethe, Nietzsche,
Rilke, and others – a starting point for much post-war literary
criticism.

Michael Hamburger, *Reason and Energy* (Routledge & Kegan Paul,
1957). Valuable introductory essays on poets by a poet.

The eight volumes in the series *German Men of Letters*, ed. Alex Natan
and Brian Keith-Smith (Oswald Wolff, 1961–) contain many useful
introductory essays on nearly 100 writers.

Period studies

W. H. Bruford, *Culture and Society in Classical Weimar, 1775–1806*
(Cambridge University Press, 1962). Consciously modelled on
Raymond Williams.

T. J. Reed, *The Classical Centre: Goethe and Weimar 1775–1832*
(Croom Helm, 1980; Oxford University Press, 1986). Stylish and
scholarly literary criticism, though unsympathetic to Hölderlin.

J. P. Stern, *Reinterpretations: Seven Studies in Nineteenth-Century
German Literature* (Thames & Hudson, 1964). Searching studies
of prose writers.

Ronald Gray, *The German Tradition in Literature 1871–1945*
(Cambridge University Press, 1965, 1977). Wide-ranging and
controversial.

J. P. Stern, *The Dear Purchase: A Theme in German Modernism*
(Cambridge University Press, 1995, 2006). Intellectual analysis of
most major 20th-century figures.

Individual writers

John Williams, *The Life of Goethe: A Critical Biography* (Blackwell,
2001).

Nicholas Boyle, *Goethe. The Poet and the Age* (Oxford University Press, 1991, 2000). Two volumes. A third is in preparation.

Lesley Sharpe, *Friedrich Schiller: Drama, Thought and Politics* (Cambridge University Press, 1991).

David Constantine, *Hölderlin* (Oxford University Press, 1988).

Nigel Reeves, *Heinrich Heine: Poetry and Politics* (Oxford University Press, 1974).

Bryan Magee, *Wagner and Philosophy* (Allen Lane, 2000).

Robert Norton, *Secret Germany: Stefan George and His Circle* (Cornell University Press, 2002).

T. J. Reed, *Thomas Mann: The Uses of Tradition*, 2nd edn (Oxford University Press, 1996).

The Cambridge Companion to Brecht, ed. Peter Thomson and Glendyr Sacks, 2nd edn (Cambridge University Press, 2007).

Julian Preece, *The Life and Work of Günter Grass: Literature, History, Politics* (Palgrave, 2001).

W. G. Sebald, A Critical Companion, ed. J. J. Long and Anne Whitehead (Edinburgh University Press, 2004).

German Literature

Index

A

absolutism 7, 10, 12, 34, 37, 39–40, 45–6, 48, 50, 59, 80, 100, 129, 143, 157
Addison, J. 38
Adenauer, K. 152
Adorno, T. 130, 139–41, 144–5, 156
aesthetics 42, 48, 66, 93, 150, see also 'Art'
Africa 18
Albert, Prince Consort 18
alexandrine 35
America see USA
Anabaptists 32
Anna Amalia, duchess of Saxe-Weimar 44
anti-Semitism 94, 101, 130
aphorism 47, 66, 102
Apollo 42
architecture 7, 113, 151, 158, Illustration 7
army 17, 21, 75, 125, 136, 139
Arnim, L.A. 74, 83
art history 9, 42
'Art' 11, 21, 42, 46, 61, 66–7, 69, 73–4, 80, 93, 97–8, 100, 104–5, 107, 112, 114–16, 120, 122, 124, 129–30, 132, 140–2, 149
Athenaeum 66
Auden, W.H. 139
Augsburg 27, 128 Peace of 32, 34
Augustine 30
Auschwitz 144–5, 150
Austria 2, 4–5, 9, 13, 19, 20, 23, 75, 96, 100

Austro-Prussian War see Seven Weeks War

B

Bakunin, M. 97
Baltic states 5
Basle 82
battle of the historians (Historikerstreit) 156
Bauer, B. 82
Baumgarten, A.G. 42
Bavaria 13, 15, 98, 104
Bayreuth 100
Beethoven, L. 80, 96
Belgium 2
Benjamin, W. 129–30, 136
Benn, G. 117, 126, 136, 144, 147
Bennett, A. 113
Berg, A. 117, 130
Berlin 71, 73–5, 81, 105, 107, 109–12, 116–17, 123, 128–9, 132–3, 136, 149–50
Bertram, E. 124
Bible 28, 30, 101, 130
'Bildung' 15–17, 21, 28, 100, 122, 133, 140, 150–1, 154, 156
'Bildungsbürger' 15, 19, 96, 100, 102, 107, 112, 114, 133–4
Bismarck, O. 5, 13–14, 16–17, 20, 22, 24, 96–8, 100, 104, 108, 110, 112, 154, Illustration 2
Black Forest 35
Blake, W. 34, 91
Böhme, J. 34
Böll, H. 151–3
Bonn 82, 124
Bonn Republic 23
bourgeois tragedy 45
bourgeoisie 8, 10, 14–17, 19–20, 22, 24, 26, 28, 34, 36–40, 45–6, 48, 51, 54–5, 58, 64, 67, 73–4, 80–1, 93–4,

bourgeoisie (*Cont.*)
96-8, 101, 104-5, 107-9,
112-15, 122-3, 126, 128,
131-3, 136, 140, 143, 149,
Illustration 9
Brahm, O. 110-11, 116
Brandenburg 5
Brant, S. 30
Bremen 38, 41
Brentano, C. 74, 83, 89
Britain, *see* England
British Empire 18, 75, 128, 158
Brockes, B.H. 39, 41
Brunswick, duke of 46
Büchner, G. 85-8, 93, 109, 111,
116, 128
Büchner, L. 93-4
Burns, R. 49
Busch, W. 94, Illustration 10

C

California 139, 141
Calvinism 32
Campo Formio, treaty 68
capital, capitalism 7-8, 10, 19-21,
37, 48, 78, 101, 110, 126,
128, 136, 138, 140
Carlsbad Decrees 12, 75
Catholicism 6, 9, 17-18, 23, 30,
34, 52-3, 73, 75, 90-1,
105, 108, 124, 132, 152
Cavell, E. 126
Celan, P. 145-8, Illustration 18
Charles V 32
chivalrous literature 28, 74
Christianity 6, 9, 60, 65, 70, 82,
84, 91, 96, 100-1
church 8-9, 18, 32-3, 36-7, 41,
46, 54, 67, 152
'civilization' 19, 120, 122, 126
'classical' period 11, 15-16, 23-24,
59-60, 89, 96, 100,
102, 104, 125, 133, 148,
Illustration 7

classics 9
clergy 5-11, 13, 67, 124
Cold War 18, 148, 154
Cologne 27
colonies 9, 18, 20, 54, 81, 112
communism 17, 21, 83, 92, 126,
128, 133, 144, 148, 150
Communist Manifesto 17
Copernicus, N. 59
copyright 15, 78, 96
Cotta, J.F. 63, 68
Courage (Courasche) 36, 138-9
courts 7, 10-11, 15, 36, 38, 40, 63,
67, 72, 75
crash of 1873 17
crash of 1929 22, 134
culture, *see* Kultur
Customs Union ('Zollverein')
13-14, 85
Czechs 21

D

Darwin, C. 94, 96, 110, 113
Dawes Plan 123
Defoe, D. 38, 40
deism 9, 45, 48
Denmark 41, 61, 137
depression 17, 22
Descartes, R. 30, 37
'Deutschland, Deutschland über
alles' 13
Dickens, C. 88
Döblin, A. 132-3, 153
Drama 11, 28, 33, 40, 45, 49-52,
54-7, 60-1, 63, 68-9, 72,
77, 87-8, 92, 97, 101, 104,
110-12, 116-17, 123-4,
128-9, 137-9, 149-51,
153
Dresden 39, 46, 61, 97, 136, 157
Droste-Hülshoff, A. 90-1, 106
dualism 30
Dürer, A. 29-30
Dürrenmatt, F. 2

E

Eckhart ('Meister Eckhart') 28, 34
education 9, 36, 61, 63–4, 66, 96, 132
Eichendorff, J. 73, 89
Eichmann, A. 22
Einstein, A. 123
emigration 17, 32, 54, 136, 142–4, 158
empires 18, 75, 77–8, 120, 132, 158
Engels, F. 17, 24, 81, 83
England, Britain 7–10, 18–19, 23, 34, 38, 80–81, 107, 120, 128, 155–6, 158
Enlightenment 9, 37–40, 45–6, 55, 58–9, 64, 66, 77, 101, 130–1, 139–41, 156
Enzensberger, H.M. 148
Erfurt 44
Eulenspiegel 28
Europe 2, 15, 27, 29, 36–9, 49, 51, 66, 69, 74–5, 104, 113–15, 122–3, 132, 139–40, 147, 149
Expressionism 123, 136

F

famine 14
Faust 33, 45–6, 49, 52–4, 64–5, 78, 85, 89, 141–2
Faust-book, *see*: *History of Dr John Faust*
feudalism 27–8, 37
Feuerbach, L. 81–3, 97
Fichte, J.G. 63, 65, 68, 71, 74–5
Fielding, J. 40, 44, 47
First World War 19, 116, 134, 142
folk-songs 28, 48–9, 74, 83, 133
Fontane, T. 107–11, 114
France 7, 8, 19, 20, 23, 25, 35, 37–8, 40, 45–6, 48–9, 62–4, 68–9, 74–5, 80–1, 84–6, 105, 120, 122, 132
Franco-Prussian War 13, 96, 100
Frankfurt 33, 35–6, 39, 48–9, 54, 74, 125, 130, 144, 150, 156
Frankfurt Parliament 13, 15, 98
Frederick II, ' the Great' 22, 46, 151
free trade 14, 17, 18
freedom 11, 32, 36, 50, 59–61, 68, 86, 94, 114, 120, 122, 140, 158
French language 38, 105
French Revolution of 1789 63–5, 69–71, 75, 78, 86, 150
French Revolution of 1830 80, 84
Freytag, G. 94–5
Friedrich II, *see* Frederick II, 'the Great'
Friedrich Wilhelm IV 13
Fromm, E. 130
Fronde 7

G

Galsworthy, J. 113
Gauss, C.F. 47
'Geistesgeschichte' 124, 129
Gelnhausen 35
genius 47–8, 52, 61, 138
George II 38
George III 47
George, S. 105–6, 124–5, 131, 136, Illustration 13
German Democratic Republic 2, 24–6, 143–4, 147–50, 154–7
German Federal Republic ('Bonn Republic') 2, 23–5, 143–4, 147–50, 153–7
Germanic Federation 13, 84
German language 2, 28, 32, 34, 40, 49–50, 75, 111, 132, 154, 158

German Mercury (Der Teutsche Merkur) 45, 63
'Germanistics' 17, 22
Germany 1–4, 12–14, 16, 21, 23, 25–7, 32, 47–8, 62, 71, 74–5, 78, 96–7, 100–1, 105, 113–15, 120, 123–5, 132, 140, 142–4, 149, 154, 156 and *passim*, Illustration 1
globalization 17, 19, 24, 26, 115–16, 120, 135, 137, 144, 156, 158
Goering, R. 123
Goethe Institutes 24
Goethe Societies 102
Goethe, J.W. 48–54, 57, 58, 61–65, 67–8, 73–4, 77–8, 80, 83, 85–90, 96, 98, 102, 104–5, 111, 124, 137, 145, 153–4, 158, Illustration 8
Goldsmith, O. 53
Göttingen 38, 40, 47
Gottsched, J.C. 39–41, 45, 49, 62
Götz von Berlichingen 49
Grass, G. 152–4, 157, Illustration 19
Greece 69, 70, 72, 105, Illustration 7
Grimm, J. 75
Grimm, W. 75
Grimmelshausen J. J. C. 35–6, 139, 153
Gropius, W. 132
Grosz, G. 126, 128
Grünbein, D. 157
Gründerzeit 92, 96
'Gruppe 47' 144
Gryphius, A. 35
Gundolf, F. 124
Gutenberg, J. 30

H

Habermas, J. 156
Hafiz 77

Hagedorn, F. 38
Halle 36
Hamburg 38–40, 46
Hanover 38, 154
Hapsburg family 32, 34
Hardenberg, F. 66, 72–3, 131
Hauptmann, G. 110–13, 136
Haydn, J. 96, 100
Hebbel, F. 92–3, 97
Hegel, G.W.F. 66, 70–1, 75, 77, 80–2, 92–3, 97
Heidegger, M. 124, 126, 132, 135, 156, Illustration 17
Heine, H. 83–5, 89, 92, 97, 110
Helen of Troy 33, 52, 65, 78
Herder, J.G. 48–9, 54, 57, 65, 74
Hesse, H. 133–4, 140–1, 144
hexameter 41, Illustration 9
Heym, G. 117
Heyse, P. 104
Historikerstreit *see* battle of the historians
History 9, 38, 48, 61, 74–5, 85, 92, 122, 124, 136, 158
History of Dr John Faust 33
Hitler, A. 2, 23–4, 135–6, 142, 150
Hochhuth, R. 149
Hoffmann von Fallersleben 13
Hoffmann, E.T.A. 73
Hoffmann, H. 94
Hölderlin, F. 65–6, 69–71, 81, 86, 106, 125–6
Holland 7, 8
'Holocaust' 22, 26, 145, 149, 156
Holy Roman Empire 5–6, 12, 13, 21, 23, 32, 38, 50, 67, 71–5
Holz, A. 109–10
Homer 41
Horae (Die Horen) 62–4, 66–8
Horkheimer, M. 130, 139–41
Humboldt, A. 65, 75
Humboldt, W. 65, 71, 75
Hume, D. 58
Hungary 2, 155

Hus, J. 32
hymns 30, 66, 69

I

Ibsen, H. 109–10
idealism 9, 57, 58–9, 64–7,
    69, 71–4, 77–8, 81, 83,
    85, 89, 92–3, 101, 104–5,
    112, 132
identity 19, 28, 30, 32, 37, 42, 67,
    69, 71–3, 91–2, 94, 116,
    132, 143, 159
Iffland, A.W. Illustration 6
Imperial Free Cities 6–7, 37, 39,
    48, 112
India 75, 105, 133
indulgences 30
industrialization, industry 14,
    18, 27, 47, 78, 81, 83, 94,
    100, 105, 109–10, 116, 123,
    126, 132
inflation 20, 122–3, 126
Institute for Social Research
    (Institut für
    Sozialforschung) 130,
    139, 144
Ireland 14
Italy 2, 13, 27, 29, 40, 62

J

James, H. 106
Jean Paul see Richter, J.P.F.
Jena 61, 63, 65–6, 68, 71–4
Jena, battle 71, 77
Jesus Christ 70, 82
Jews 17, 22, 84–5, 91, 94, 96, 105,
    117, 130, 131–2, 136, 145,
    149–50, 156
Johnson, U. 155, 158
Joyce, J. 132, 154
Jünger, E. 125–6, 132, 136, 156
Junkers 12, 17–18

K

Kafka, F. 4
Kaiser, G. 123
Kant, I. 58–9, 61, 63–4, 68–70,
    72, 122
Karl August, duke of
    Saxe-Weimar 45, 54, 61,
    63
Kerr, A. 136
Kerr, J. 136
Kleist, H. 72, 81, 87
Klinger, F.M. 55
Klopstock, F.G. 41–2, 50–1
Kohl, H. 156–7
Kommerell, M. 125
Königsberg 58, 63
'Kultur' 19, 48, 63, 73, 97, 100,
    112, 115, 120, 131, 133,
    135, 142
'Kulturkampf' 18

L

Lasker-Schüler, E. 117–18, 145
Latin 7, 36, 41
League of Nations 135
*Leaves for Art (Blätter für die
    Kunst)* 105
Leibniz, G.W. 37–40, 44, 48,
    58, 82
Leipzig 39, 41, 45–6, 48, 61, 81
Leisewitz, J.A. 55
Lenz, J.M.R. 49, 53–4, 61, 85–7,
    111–12
Lessing, G.E. 45–6, 49, 51,
    59–60, 96
liberalism 14, 21, 93, 131, 136
Lichtenberg, G.C. 8, 47
Liechtenstein 2
literacy 6, 28, 33, 73, 81, 88, 92
Locke, J. 37
London 27, 107, 136
Louis XIV 7, 40

Lübeck 112–13
Ludwig II 98–100, Illustration 11
Luther, M. 30–3, 49, 137
Lutheranism 5, 11, 32–6, 54, 60,
    65, 70, 92, 97, 124
Luxembourg 2

M

Mainz 30
Mallarmé, S. 105
Mandeville, B. 37
Mann, H. 112, 116, 120, 136,
    Illustration 15
Mann, T. 112–16, 120–2,
    130–2, 141–2, 144, 154,
    Illustration 15
Mannheim, 60–1
Marcuse, H. 130
Marlowe, C. 33
Marx, K., Marxism 17, 24, 81–3,
    85, 93, 97, 128–30, 136,
    138–9, 150
Mastersingers 28, 98
materialism 15, 24, 37, 44, 55,
    57, 81, 89, 101, 106, 110,
    129, 131
Mechthild von Magdeburg 28
Middle Ages 4, 6, 30, 48–9, 66,
    74–5, 77, 100
Milton, J. 41
Mitscherlich, A. and M. 142–4
modern languages 9, 65
modernity 1, 9, 19–21, 65, 69–71,
    78, 84, 88, 97, 100–1, 110,
    126, 128, 132–3, 140, 148
monad 37, 44, 48, 54
monetarization 28, 30
moral weeklies 38
Morgenstern, C. 118–19
Mörike, E. 88–91, 106
Moroccan Crisis 117
Müller, H. 150–1
Munich 104–7, 112, 114, 116,
    141

music 18–19, 22, 68, 73, 96–101,
    105, 130–1, 133–4, 141
mysticism 28, 30, 34, 36, 105,
    133

N

Namibia 2
Napoleon 12, 67, 71, 77, 84
National Socialism 21–23, 125,
    130, 131–4, 140–4, 151–3,
    155, 157
nationalism 21, 71, 75, 78, 100,
    106, 116, 135, 156
natural sciences 9, 38, 47, 65, 93,
    96, 101, 131
navy 18
Neuschwanstein Illustration 11
new sobriety (Neue Sachlichkeit)
    124
Newton, I. 34, 37
*Nibelungs, Lay of the
    (Nibelungenlied)* 75, 97
Nietzsche, F. 81–3, 100–4, 106,
    113, 115, 117, 125–6, 131,
    133, 136, 141, 151
Nobel Prize for Literature 104,
    112, 130, 144, 153
Novalis *see* Hardenberg
novel 1, 10–11, 33, 35, 40, 44–5,
    47, 50–2, 64, 66–7, 69,
    73, 77, 94, 107–9, 112–14,
    116, 131–4, 140–2, 150–4,
    157–8
novella ('Novelle') 104–5, 107
Nuremberg 27, 98

O

Oberlin, J.F. 86
ode 35, 41, 49, 51, 69
officials 6, 8–12, 14–15, 17, 19–20,
    22, 24, 26, 37–40, 44, 48,
    51, 55, 58–9, 63–4, 66–7,
    72–3, 77, 80, 85, 93–6,

101, 104–5, 112, 114–16,
118, 122, 124, 128, 131–6,
142–3
opera 7, 40, 97–100, 117, 127–9
Opitz, M. 34–5, 39
'Ostalgie' 26
'other Germany' 23, 24

P

Paraguay 81
Paris 84–5, 88, 92, 97, 105, 107
Philology 9, 65, 75
Philosophy 9, 11, 19, 25, 34, 37–9,
44, 58–61, 64–6, 70, 72,
74, 81–5, 92–3, 96–8,
101–2, 105, 113–15, 124,
130, 132, 139, 156
Pietism 34, 36, 42, 44, 50
Pindar 69
poetry 1, 25, 35, 39–42, 49–50,
53, 61–2, 66–7, 69–71,
73–5, 77, 83–5, 88–92, 94,
96, 104–7, 110, 114–15,
117–19, 123, 125–9, 136–7,
141, 144–9, 153, 157
Poland 2, 5, 20, 34, 48, 115, 153
population 7, 14, 27, 73, 88, 122–3
Pound, E. 65
Prague 7, 155
princes 6–7, 11–12, 27, 32, 34–5,
39, 42, 46–7, 50, 52, 54–5,
57, 61–2, 97, 110, 112, 124,
140, 143
printing 6, 30, 33, 36, 41, 63,
78, 105
proletarianization 21, 24, 126,
132
protectionism 17–18, 22, 116, 135
Protestantism 9–10, 34, 45, 73,
124, *see also* Lutheranism,
Reformation
Proudhon, P.J. 97
Prussia 5, 9, 12–15, 18, 21, 23–24,
46, 71–5, 78, 94, 105,

107–9, 114–16, 122, 151,
157
Prussian Academy 136
psychology 19, 130, 142
publishing 8–9, 36, 39–41, 62–3,
67, 81, 94, 96, 136

R

Rabelais, F. 30
Racine, J. 40
radio 25, 134, 136
railways 14, 133, 158
Rathenau, W. 130
realism 10, 30, 36, 44, 46–7,
50–3, 67, 85, 104, 107–15,
123, 139
Reformation 5–6, 23, 33, *see also*
Luther
Reichstag 16, 32, 134
Reinhart, M. 116
Remarque, E. 139
ressentiment 101
Restoration 77, 84
're-unification' 157
Revolution of 1848 13–15, 80, 85,
92–3, 97–8, 112–13
Revolution of 1918 20, 122–3, 149
Reynard the Fox 29
Richardson, S. 40, 45, 52
Richter, J.P.F. 67, 73
Riemenschneider, T. 29,
Illustration 3
Romanticism 15, 66, 72–4, 77,
83–5, 91, 97, 116, 131,
Illustration 9
Rome 6, 32, 42, 62
Russia 5, 21, 24, 97, 120, 139,
143–4, 157

S

Sachs, H. 28, 49, 98
Saxe-Weimar 45, 54, 68, 77

Schelling, F.W.J. 66–7, 70–2
Schiller, F. 55–7, 60–6, 68–70, 72, 77, 86, 90, 96–7, 102–4, 112, 149
Schinkel, C.F. Illustration 7
Schlaf, J. 109–10
Schlegel, A.W. 66, 75, 77
Schlegel, F. 66, 72, 75, 77
Schmidt, A. 154
Schmitt, C. 132
Schopenhauer, A. 81–3, 93, 98–101, 113, 131
Scotland 37–8
Scott, W. 50
Sebald, W.G. 157–8
Second Empire (Reich) 5, 14, 16–19, 21–3, 93, 102, 105, 107, 112, 114, 118, 131, 141, 149, 153, Illustrations 1, 2
Secularization 11, 48, 60, 66
Sentimentalism (Empfindsamkeit) 44–5, 50–2, 54, 67–8
Seven Weeks War (1866) 13, 96
Seven Years War 9, 45
Shakespeare, W. 44–5, 48–50, 66, 68
Silesia 34–5, 46, 73, 94, 105, 110–11, 136
social security 18, 25
socialism 17, 21, 97, 101, 122, 126, 133, 139, 143, 150–2, 155–6
Socialist Unity Party 24
sonnet 35
Sophocles 69
Spengler, O. 122, 126, 136
Spitzweg, C. Illustration 9
St Petersburg 107
state 6–11, 14–15, 17–18, 20–1, 26, 32–3, 36, 38–9, 41, 46, 59, 64, 67, 71–5, 81, 92, 94, 97–8, 112, 114–16, 122–3, 125, 128, 136, 149

'state socialism' 18, 20–1, 26
Sterne, L. 44, 47, 67
Storm and Stress (Sturm und Drang) 49, 54, 57, 64, 74, 85, 107, 129
Storm, T. 105
Strasbourg 35, 48–50
Strauss, D.F. 81–2, 88, 96–7, 100–1
Strauss, L. 132
Stuttgart 55, 63, 81, 88
swastika 105, 125
Switzerland 2, 4, 8, 41, 54, 97, 133, 144

T

theatre 11, 33, 38, 40–1, 46, 60, 63–4, 68, 92, 97, 110–11, 116, 123–4, 129, 136, 140, 147, 149–51
theology 8–11, 25, 28, 30, 34, 36, 41–2, 45–6, 48, 54, 60–1, 65, 70, 73, 82, 92–3, 101, 110
Third Empire (Reich) 5, 22, 134–6, 142–3, 150, 153, 155, 157
Thirty Years War 7, 34–5, 138–9, 143, 153
Tieck, J.L. 73, 104
Toller, E. 123, 136
towns 6–8, 27–35, 49, 55, 57, 88, 112, 137, 151, 157
tragedy 35, 40, 45–7, 53–4, 60–62, 65, 68–9, 72, 82, 86–8, 97, 101, 128, 138
Triple Entente 120
Tübingen 65, 82, 88, 93
turn (Wende) 157–8
Twilight of Humanity (Menschheitsdämmerung) 123, 126

U

university 7, 9, 11, 13, 15, 17, 22,
 24–5, 30, 36, 38–41, 44,
 48, 51–2, 55, 57–9, 61, 63,
 65, 67, 70–1, 75, 81–2, 86,
 94, 96, 114, 124, 130, 135,
 140, 158, Illustration 17
USA 23, 26, 54, 61, 116, 123, 126,
 128, 130, 139–41, 143, 147,
 155–6, 158

V

Vergangenheitsbewältigung 143
Verlaine, P. 105
Versailles 20, 125, Illustration 2
versification 35, 49, 60, 62,
 66, 97, 105, 149, *see also*
 hexameter
Virgil 41
visual arts 6, 19, 22, 29, 42, 46,
 62, 84, 97, 105, 129, 132,
 153, Illustration 7
Vulpius, C. 63
Wagner, H.L. 49, 53
Wagner, R. 97–101, 104, 112, 131
Wall 24, 143, 154, 156
Wedekind, F. 116–17, 129
Weill, K. 128
Weimar 45, 54, 61–2, 67–8, 73,
 77, 98, 102–4, 122, 124,
 132
Weimar Republic 5, 20–1, 122,
 124, 126, 129–33, 137, 141
Weiss, P. 150

Wende *see* turn
Werner, Z. 77
Westphalia, Peace of 34
White Mountain, battle 34
Wieland, C.M. 43–5, 50, 54, 63,
 65, Illustration 5
Wilde, O. 11
Wilhelm II 111, 122
Wilhelm I 13, Illustration 2
Winckelmann, J.J.W. 42, 62, 70,
 72, 97
Wittenberg 30
Wolf, C. 155, 157
Wolf, H. 89
Wolfenbüttel 46, 59
Wolff, C.A. 38–40, 42, 58–9
women 17, 28, 44, 67, 90–2
work 19, 22, 28, 30, 48, 94,
 109–11, 117, 122–3, 125–6,
 130, 136, 143, 147
Worms 32
writers 8, 10, 28, 37, 48, 54, 72,
 80, 90, 96, 104–5, 112,
 115, 136, 144
Württemberg 60, 65, 133, 149

Y

Young Germany (Junges
 Deutschland) 84, 86, 97

Z

Zola, E. 109
Zollverein *see* Customs Union
Zurich 82, 86, 137

Index